U.S. Church Planting in the 2020s with an extended discussion of what can and cannot be emulated from the Chinese house church movement, highlights of the Church Plant Survivability and Health Study of 2007, a Denominational Sampling of Church Planting Techniques, Critiques of the Missional and Emergent Church Movement and a Look at Urban Church Planting in Global Cities

Dr. Brian D. Farley, D.Min.
Trinity Theological Seminary, Evansville, IN

Church Planting in the 2020s

*Starting Churches in a Rapidly
Changing Culture*

Dr. Brian D. Farley

Copyright © 2020

Brian Farley Ministries Incorporated, New York, NY

No portion of this book may be distributed or copied digitally or in print without the express, written permission of the author and/or the entity Brian Farley Ministries Inc.

Contents

Dedication xi
Thank you xv
Learning from Success and Failure xix

Part I Spiritual Considerations, Warfare, Miracles, and Church Business 1

Chapter 1 The Spiritual Side of Church Planting 3
    1.1 The Critical Need for American Church Planting Today 3
    1.2: Calling, Convictions, and Categories of Church Planters and Plants 4
    1.3 The Firm Foundation of Jesus Christ, the Cornerstone of the Church 8
    1.4 The Cornerstone of the Church 11

Chapter 2 Modern Spirit Filled Churches, Spirit Warfare in Church Planting and Miracles 16
    2.1 The Modern Spirit-Filled Church 16
    2.2 Opposition and Spiritual Warfare in Church Planting and Church Revitalization 25
    2.3 The Place of Miracles in Church Planting 33

                  2.4 The result of this experience- Opposition leads to Victory 44

Chapter 3 Getting Down to Business Legally and Practically . 51
                  3.1 The Business Side of Church Planting - Legal and Financial Considerations 51
                  3.2 Mission Statements, Vision Statements and Core Values 61
                  3.3 Forming a Launch Team 76
                  3.4 Church Member Leadership Roles 82
                  3.5 Church Marketing 85
                  3.6 Staffing 90

PART II CHURCH PLANTING MODELS, CHINESE HOUSE CHURCHES AND DENOMINATIONAL APPROACHES 93

Chapter 4 Church Planting Models and Movement 95
                  4.1 Overview of Five Types of Church Planting Models and Movements 96
                  4.2 The Traditional Model 96
                  4.3 The Large Launch/Attractional Model 98
                  4.4 Missional Incarnational/Emergent Church Planting 100
                  4.5 House/Simple/Organic Churches 102
                  4.6 Multi-site or Campus Churches 105

Chapter 5 Five Facts about Chinese House Churches 108
                  House Churches: Breaking the Secret Chinese Formula of Success 108

5.1 Fact #1- Chinese house churches have experienced major and serious persecution for years 111

5.2 Fact #2- Chinese house churches are most frequently Pentecostal and/or Charismatic in nature, relying heavily on the supernatural with obvious manifestation of spiritual gifts as the norm, not the exception 113

5.3 Fact #3- Super successful Chinese house churches participated in a form of multi-level marketing type training for new believers and leaders 115

5.4 Fact #4- The Mega Success of Chinese house churches occurred and occurs primarily in rural areas 119

5.5 Fact #5- Chinese house church movements were started by deeply committed men and women of God who burned with passion for the Lord and called others to wake from their spiritual stupor 123

Chapter 6 Denominational Models and Approaches Sampler 126
    6.1 Anabaptist/Mennonite/Brethren Church 126
    6.2 An Episcopal Church Planting Perspective 130
    6.3 An Evolving United Methodist Church 133
    6.4 The Southern Baptist Convention 137
    6.5 The Growing Assemblies of God 139

Part III The Church Plant Study, Missional/Emergent Churches, Urban Planting & Breaking Barriers for Small Churches 141

Chapter 7 The Church Plant Survivability Study of 2007 143
    7.1 Factors Associated with higher Attendance and Baptism Counts: 144
    7.2 First Year Insights 145
    7.3 Facilities Insights 146
    7.4 Funding, Planter Compensation/Benefits and Church Receipts 147
    7.5 Four Factors Associated with Church Plant Higher Attendances 150
    7.6 Four Factors Associated with Church Plant Survivability 153

Chapter 8 Arguments Against the Missional and Emergent Church Movements 158
    8.1 Missional and Emergent Church Movements 158
    8.2 Arguments Against the Missional Incarnational/ Emergent Church Approach 161
    8.3 Church Membership is Not Irrelevant Today 162
    8.4 Church Services Still Serve a Unique Purpose in Society 163
    8.5 Religious Church Buildings Can Set the Tone for Worship 165
    8.6 Denominations and Movements Must Institutionalize if They are to Last 168

Chapter 9 Urban Church Planting 172
    9.1 Urban Church planting and specifically in New York City 172
    9.2 A Model for Urban Church Planting: Barquisimeto, Venezuela 173
    9.3 Global and Urban City Church Planting Considerations: language/ethnicity and real estate challenges 175

Chapter 10 Breaking Church Growth Attendance Barriers for the Small Church 183
    10.1- Pastor, Quit being the primary or only caregiver 184
    10.2- Pastor, Quit literally doing almost everything. 190
    10.3 Get People Involved in Doing Something (Anything that is Good and Productive). 193
    10.4 If you lean to being a perfectionist (or at least excellence) in pastoring and ministry - then quit being so concerned with quality and get more concerned with quantity. 195
    10.5 Read and Pay Great Attention to the Book, How to Break Growth Barriers 198

Bibliography 201

DEDICATION

This book is dedicated to the men and women who strive to establish churches, those who help them accomplish this, and the pastors who have the guts to take an old, 90% dead, established-church and believe by faith to turn it around. This project is dedicated to the guys who believe that Jesus' name needs to be presented in a manner that is worthy of His Power and Majesty. To the people who give up great jobs to work harder than they ever have in their life, even though they may not see much fruit for 10 years, or at all in this life. To the people who pastor the church that the superintendent/bishop/associational leader couldn't talk anybody into taking, but somehow they decided to "just fill in" for one more week until the weeks became months, and they could not get that problem little church out of their spirit. This book is dedicated to the church planter who cuts the grass, cleans the sanctuary, and prints the bulletin (they know they shouldn't, they know they can't do everything, but they could not let it - not get done). This book is dedicated to the guy who picks up trash in the churchyard on Saturday night at 10 p.m. before Easter service the next day and visits five people in the hospital after church on Easter Sunday afternoon. This book is dedicated to the good pastors who are determined that the Church is worth giving our very best and loving our very best. We are not called just to take a salary and a parsonage, but we are called to expand the Kingdom and storm hell with a squirt gun if necessary. This book is dedicated to those pastors who will not sit idly by as other religions and cults take our cities while we continually move only to the suburbs to build nice churches while the city is given to enemies of the Gospel. This book is dedicated to the small-town pastor who faithfully serves in a place that may never be recognized by anyone, but God. This book is dedicated to those who are sold out to share the love and power of Jesus with a confused generation in a lost and dying world. This book is dedicated to pastors who are passionately seeking to turn the tide in these last days before the soon return of our Lord and Savior, Jesus Christ, who will soon establish His Kingdom and set right all that is wrong.

Introductory Comments

THANK YOU

This book would not be possible without the tireless support of Heather Farley. After 26+ years of marriage and ministry, she has stood by my side and supported me through easy and difficult seasons of ministry and life. Many ministries have been derailed or crippled by unsupportive pastor's wives, but Heather serves faithfully with me and she is 100% involved in the work of the Church. Heather has spent many nights entertaining herself while I was involved in an online seminary class or away at an onsite seminar class. Heather has never complained as funds were spent on ministerial education while she went without many wants. Heather has been supportive of this whole process from beginning to end, and the work would not have been completed without her unending support and love. Thank you for being my Valentine, Best Friend, Greatest Supporter, Mother of my children, Minister of Music, Pastor's Wife, and soooo much more. Thank you so much to my awesome wife and ministry partner, Heather.

This book would not have been complete without my parents Dr. Dale and Paulette Farley, who have always lovingly supported me. Thank you to my father as well for always encouraging me to pursue further education and supporting me in these efforts. Thanks to my mother for her unending support and love.

Thank you to my children, Aaron Joel (Hannah) and Andrew Micah, for loving me and understanding when the ministry demands were great. We are very proud of you and believe God is going to use you both to do great things for His Kingdom and pleasure. You are loved more than you can currently understand (until you have your own children). We are also very thankful for God bringing Hannah Farley into our life and recognize her as a great gift of God for Aaron.

I thank the Church and the church members that I have pastored through the years. Thank you for your patience with me as I am sometimes a "spaz" and have made many mistakes along the way. Thank you for working with us as we built the Kingdom of God together. Thank you to the churches that allowed us to minister to you while traveling.

Additionally, thanks go to - Bishop Mike Gray (Alpha Conference, Montgomery, Alabama) who patiently served as my bishop for seven years and walked with me through some difficult situations, gave me the opportunity to pastor Faith Chapel and led me as a conference executive council member. Bishop David Stephens who served as my bishop for more than nine years, gave me the opportunity to pastor what would become Harvest Christian Center, walked with me through many interesting church situations, allowed me to serve full-time in the conference office, placed me as the conference youth camp director and has served as a friend in many ways. Bishop Garry Bryant allows me the distinct privilege of itinerating throughout the International Pentecostal Holiness Church as a traveling minister operating under the auspices of Evangelism USA. Presiding IPHC Bishop, Dr. Doug Beacham also has graciously spoken into our lives on more than one occasion and has been very kind to us for which we are thankful. Bishop Tony Miller of The Gate Church, OKC, OK, has also graciously encouraged us when speaking prophecy over us and then being very generous to us in the last year. The Executive Council of Mission New York (Rev. Rick Fountain, Pastor Tim Nail, and Pastor Kirk Walters) are very kind to me and put in many hours assisting with the administrative side of the ministry. These men on the council also travel to make meetings happen, often paying their own way and are generally a blessing. Assistant Bishop Doug Bartlett of the North Carolina Conference of the IPHC is one of our largest supporters and encouragers as the conference director for the NC IPHC Missions and Evangelism Department. Rev. Doug Bartlett has been a super encouragement and connector that, without his help, the mission may have already failed. A special thank you also goes to Dr. Terry Tramel and Bishop Talmadge Gardner for graciously letting Mission New York be included in Great Commission Meals, which without that exposure, we would not have been able to be successful in booking many of the churches we are connected to today. We are also very grateful for Bishops: Greg Amos, Tim Lamb, David Moore, Manuel Pate, Danny Nelson, Ray Willis. Each of these Bishops graciously allows us to itinerate in their respective territories of the IPHC. While many pastors have helped us, we must specifically mention the over the top help of a good friend, Pastor Tim Nail, Lake City, SC. We cannot forget the host of encouragers in the leadership and the laity of the International Pentecostal Holiness Church. A special thanks also goes to all the pastors and members of the IPHC and many other churches (Assembly of God, Church of God, Non-denominational, Charismatic, Independent and United Methodist) which have faithfully supported us with your prayers, opening your pulpits and financial support. Without our monthly financial and prayer partners, there would be no Mission New York.

Additionally, from earlier in ministry, we appreciate Pastors Sherrill Isbell, Ernest L. Quinley and Don Price who all opened doors for us as a new minister and then granted associate roles at a large church and a mega-church. Pastor Fred Watson also blessed us with one of our first full-time senior pastor appointments when he served as a district overseer.

Of course, I thank God for the Lord Jesus Christ, the Father, and the precious Holy Spirit. Without the shedding of Christ' Blood for us on the cross of Calvary, without Jesus, there would be no Church or lasting, eternal hope of glory. Thank you, Jesus, to the only One worthy of our praise. I praise You for who You are. I thank you for Your faithfulness, power, comfort, healing and the thousands of other incredible things you have done for us. Jesus is worthy of all praise!

As many have said before, I agree that Jesus has truly been better to me than I have been to myself.

LEARNING FROM SUCCESS AND FAILURE

Sometimes in the circles I run, I may be considered a very small bit of a ministerial success. While the Lord has never used me to build a megachurch, He has helped us to build a church that eventually reached a few hundred people. In 2000, the Lord helped us start a church with 11 people that later took over another extremely small church. In the years that followed, the Lord helped us baptize 258 believers, build two new buildings, totally rebuild another building after a direct hit by a major hurricane and expand the churches' land holdings as well. In just under 14 years, the Lord helped us: eventually have three weekend services, raise up 14 biblically operating elders and deacons, lead up to 20 small groups, at the peak have 22 musicians involved, have a youth group which ministered to well over 100 teens every Wednesday night, almost another 100 kids in Royal Rangers and M-Pact girls clubs, employ up to nine people including full-time youth pastors, associate pastors, and office staff, have a very large food distribution ministry, begin a school of ministry with 40 students, and see a group of 11 people grow to about 300 people all the time with special services and events reaching more than 700 and a one-time peak of over 1,400 people through the doors for Christmas services. Five years after leaving, by the grace of God, that church is not where it once was numerically, but it has an incredible pastor, over 150 people attending and is growing again.

While there are so many churches that are much larger, this church was what many, if not, most pastors would call somewhat successful. It is a situation that I like to talk about a lot when I talk about ministry. It's the one that in my own small way, my flesh is tempted to brag about as if I was personally responsible for the good things that only God could do. It is how I like to remember my ministry thus far. Then there are the situations that I do not want to talk about. The situations that remind me that you can do nothing lasting without God's grace. The situations that remind me, it's all about Jesus and certainly not about me… I have planted other churches as well. I don't talk about them very much because they do not exist. They existed in my mind at one time, but they never became a reality. In Montgomery, Alabama, I have tried to start a church twice (separated by 18 years' time). The first time I tried to start a church there, I was only 21 years old. Fresh out of the Air Force, I was young and arrogant. I knew that when people heard I was starting a church, that surely hundreds, if not thousands would quickly attend. No one could present Jesus as clearly as me, and with five years of ministry experience (I started being a youth pastor at age 16), surely I knew all I could ever need to know about church planting! I had been blessed to have a youth group in a church of about 150 that had 30-40 youth most of the time and sometimes had reached over 70 teens. Surely, we could have 50 people in no time at all!

The reality was harshly different. The reality was that in several months time of having "church services," we never had more than 13 people, and we were thrilled to have 13 people then. I knew nothing about mail-outs, the importance of location, "critical mass" (the amount of people needed to at all "feel" like a church), clueless to the money needed to successfully start a church and the list of my ignorance goes on and on and on. You don't normally start a successful church with zero funding. You don't normally start a church with no plan. You don't normally start a successful church without talented launch team members who can support you with tithes, attendance, gifting, emotional and spiritual support. You don't rent a hotel conference room in the upstairs of a hotel in a bad part of town and expect people to magically come, but at the time, this all made perfect sense to me. After 3-4 months of this, we had, had enough, and we took a youth pastor job several hundred miles away. Thank God for a gracious and understanding wife!

Now, many years later, after 14 years of relative success at church planting, surely, I was ready to go at it again. This time, things would be different. This time, I was older and wiser, but still less than 40. This time, a denomination would fund it extremely well. This time, some old church friends would help me with it (after all, surely after the successful church plant they had witnessed, this new venture would be successful). This time, we would have a plan!

The only problem was, it didn't work. We never got to launch day. For months, a very small group of people I had inherited from a closed-down church where I was once youth pastor, fought me constantly and vigorously (not all of them, but some of them - some were incredibly supportive). For months, we knew our youngest son was going to be accepted to a special magnet school for gifted students which was similar to the one we had moved him from in Florida, the only thing was, after thinking he would, he did not and almost failed 9th grade waiting to get in. The search for a suitable meeting place for the church was vigorous. I looked every day and saw hundreds of places, but none of them would work out - even though I had an amazing amount of funds at my disposal to secure them. Eventually, a millionaire decided to give me an old, run-down bank building, but the group I was a part of sent a property committee that would not allow me to accept the free building. This committee did not want a church in that part of town.

Fortunately, one thing was going right! We had signed on a home purchase and were waiting for it to close for several months. The day before we were to close on the house, the bank called and said there had been a mistake, and even though I had good credit and all the needed funds to close, they were not able to close. We were living in this house (renting it) and because of this, we had 7 days or so to move out. The denomination not accepting the free bank building and the mortgage bank denying our loan (literally within 24 hours of closing after we had it secured for several months) were both within a week of each other.

The next day, I visited a former bishop who was in the hospital, going through an extensive surgery to remove a life-threatening cancerous tumor. While at the hospital, it was made clear to me that a flagship church that had been discussed with me several months earlier was still available. Within a few weeks, we moved to that city and accepted that pastorate. This pastorate, had mixed results with some success/failure. It was a revitalization situation. The church grew but simultaneously lost 36 members to death over the course of a little more than three years. This situation taught me much about Jesus' teaching on old wineskins. I did some things right concerning revitalization (and did leave the church somewhat better numerically than when it was given to me), but I could have handled a lot of things better. It is unfortunate that a class and book from my doctorate "Strategic Planning for the Local Church" and the book "Strategic Planning for Public and Non-Profit Organizations" by John M. Bryson was not discovered by me until a year after leaving this pastorate. (It lays out an incredible plan to slowly turn the tide of old organization over the course of a few years, hopefully without losing much of what is already in place).

Like most people, it was not during the "successful" seasons of ministry that I learned the most valuable lessons. Sometimes I wonder what I can even learn from the pastors who seem to have the ministry Midas touch, and everything they touch turns to ministry gold. It was in the time of failure, humbling, and loss that I learned the most.

If you are looking to start or revitalize a church, there is a good chance you have already experienced some ministry successes and failures. If you will allow Him, God will use the experiences we have on both ends of the spectrum to teach us, mold us more into His image, and make us a willing vessel for His Kingdom service. It is my prayer that my personal ministry failures and successes, the formal study I have embarked upon concerning church planting and revitalization, and the hundreds of visits to local churches as an itinerant preacher might help someone be better prepared to plant a church or turn around an old, dying congregation.

PART I

SPIRITUAL CONSIDERATIONS, WARFARE, MIRACLES, AND CHURCH BUSINESS

CHAPTER 1

THE SPIRITUAL SIDE OF CHURCH PLANTING

1.1 The Critical Need for American Church Planting Today

I have spent the majority of my ministry (29 years at the time of this writing) in two Trinitarian-Pentecostal denominations in the southeastern United States. One of the district groups I was a part of had around 450 churches in the mid-1990s. Today they have somewhere around 375 in that same local group of churches. The other group I have been a part of either has less churches than about 20 years ago or very nearly the same number (around 50). These types of statistics seem to be plaguing many American Evangelical Church groups today. They are common in many of the districts and conferences of churches that I am familiar with in 2019. Do the superintendents/bishops, associational leaders, denominational and network supervisors care less or feel less of an urgency to reach the lost than the Church leaders of the past? Perhaps, but I don't see it.

Many, if not most, of these groups, are served by dedicated and vibrant leaders. One of these groups that have lost many churches over the last two decades was served by a "super" leader who recently built a church from scratch to several thousand. The other leaders

I know in these capacities seem to spend their best energy and individual, God-given skills and gifts in the pursuit of transforming their churches' plights. One bishop is known by those closest to him, for fervently praying for up to 2-3 hours a day. Other administrative dynamos pray some and seem to work 12 hours a day, 6 days a week. Yet, the results are not seeming to change.

While no one has all the answers to the declining Church problem in America, we can see there is a problem. We know if churches are closing in record numbers, we need to reverse this trend. The two-fold strategy of church planting (replacing dying churches with new vibrant ones) and church revitalization (stopping old churches from dying in the first place) is needed to turn this tide. While the Gospel of Jesus Christ never changes, new strategies and paradigms will be needed to reach a lost and dying world in the years to come before Jesus returns. May this book assist someone toward those ends.

1.2: Calling, Convictions, and Categories of Church Planters and Plants

While many people are "called to preach" or even "called to pastor," the calling of Church Planter or Church Revitalizer are very distinct, specific, individualized callings.

> *And He Himself gave some to be apostles, some prophets, some evangelists, and some pastors and teachers, for the equipping of the saints for the work of ministry, for the edifying of the body of Christ*, Ephesians 4:11,12 (New King James Version).

Within the five-fold ministry, we have the offices of apostle, prophet, evangelist, pastor, and teacher. While many in the conservative, Evangelical world do not even recognize the offices of apostle and prophet, most of every church group will acknowledge a gigantic contrast among the offices of the evangelist, pastor, and teacher. The evangelist, and even possibly the teacher, are not the role of pastor. "Pastor" comes from the word shepherd in the sense of someone who keeps, cares for and feeds animals. The word is used by God to describe people who will lead His "Sheep" or the people of God.

In a more modern sense, "Pastor" implies a leadership mantle of the local church. While a good argument can be made that the pastor should not be doing everything in the local church, often he does much more than the idea of Acts 6 where the first deacons were called, in order to free up the apostles, so they might be able to give themselves "continually to prayer and the ministry of the word."

> *Therefore, brethren, seek out from among you seven men of good reputation, full of the Holy Spirit and wisdom, whom we may appoint over this business; but we will give ourselves continually to prayer and to the ministry of the word." Acts 6:3,4 (New King James Version).*

As a church becomes established and healthy, hopefully, it will move toward this Biblical model of Acts 6, where the pastor is concentrating on the spiritual needs of the church. He or she is freed up to do so by the members of the church taking responsibility for the day to day business of the church and the ministries, like distribution of food, as mentioned in Acts 6.

The pastor does not just preach or teach and then move on to the next town, but the pastor is with the people. In the reality of most of today's established churches, the "pastor" will also perform a variety of both complex and seemingly unrelated tasks. The smaller the church, the more a pastor will be expected to do. A good pastor will often, realistically be expected to do a vast array of tasks: preach/

teach, care for the church building, have a strong personal and professional prayer life, care for the sick, perform weddings, funerals, baby dedications and baptisms, lead council meetings, manage his own family well, train disciples, manage the finances and the list goes on and on and on. The job is complicated and not for the faint of heart! While the evangelist and teacher's jobs tend to be more specialized, the pastor, especially of a church of less than 200 in regular attendance, will usually need to be a broad generalist. In the very, very small church, the role (while it shouldn't be) sometimes even includes cutting the churches' grass and cleaning the building!

The general role of a pastor in an average, relatively healthy, and established church is a BIG role to fill. These roles of Church Planting Pastor and Church Revitalization Pastor are that much more complicated and specialized.

The Planter Pastor - the effective church planting pastor ideally will have most or all of the above-mentioned skills, but he must also be (or at least temporarily become) a people magnet, a great administrator, a great entrepreneur, and a great vision castor. The Planting Pastor is called to make something out of nothing. He must be like God in the sense that he speaks and brings things from nothing into being. The Planting Pastor must operate quickly and decisively. The church is often compared to a ship. In the case of the planting pastor, there is no ship. You may picture a pastor whittling out a tree trunk to make a canoe, but this will not do. For the new church to survive, the new church will need to be a speed boat with a large motor onboard to push through the tumultuous waves of the upstart. A key to starting the new church will be to make decisions wisely, but also quickly in order to bring more people into the Kingdom at the fastest possible rate. The planting pastor has the luxury of not being burdened with existing church members' objections since they do not exist. At the same time, the planting pastor does not have the existing church member's finances, so new members must be found very quickly to finance the vision.

The Revitalizing Pastor - the effective revitalizing pastor will ideally have most or all of the above-mentioned skills, but he must also be (or at least temporarily become) a great people person, have the patience of Job (with existing church people) and be able to see the good in often bad and disheartening situations. The Revitalizing Pastor is called to bring dead things to life again. He must be like God in the sense that he must be a Great Counselor to the people of God. He must be a brilliant and wise leader to often difficult people. He can see where the "big ship" of the local church needs to go, yet has the ability to turn the wheel very slowly and deliberately so as not to tilt the boat so much that in turning too quickly, it takes on so much water that it sinks in the process of the turn. A key here will be to turn the big, established boat S-L-O-W-L-Y.[1]

Before someone sets out to start a church or revitalize an existing older congregation that is in trouble, it would be wise to examine their gift sets closely and determine if God has called them to these difficult tasks. One must ask themselves, "I am cut out with the unique set of skills needed to be effective in these roles?" The pastor is a unique calling within the five-fold ministry, and the role of the church planter and church revitalizer are further specialized in this field of ministry. Whatever the subcategory, inside that of the larger role of pastoring (leading an established, relatively healthy church, planting a new church or revitalizing a dying church) - all three roles of the pastor have some common foundations and characteristics that should be found in all Christian church leaders.

---

[1] This is possibly a quote from Dr. Mark Rutland or another wise man, but I cannot find the citation, so I leave this note in an attempt at honesty and proper credit.

1.3 The Firm Foundation of Jesus Christ, the Cornerstone of the Church

> *Jesus replied, " 'You must love the Lord your God with all your heart, all your soul, and all your mind.' This is the first and greatest commandment. A second is equally important: 'Love your neighbor as yourself.' The entire law and all the demands of the prophets are based on these two commandments." Matthew 22:37-40 New Living Translation*

Do I believe in the Lord Jesus Christ with all my heart?
Do I want to please Him with everything that is within me?
Am I willing to lay down my desires in order to do His will for my life?

The conversation about becoming a pastor, starting a church, or leading a church in any way should not start with leadership, buildings, organizations, and not even the plans for discipleship. The conversation should start with, "Why am I doing this?" or "Who am I doing this for?" Many pastors get caught up in leadership techniques and church growth. These things can be very beneficial to the Kingdom of God, but our first reason for starting or leading a church in any capacity should be because Jesus has loved us enough to die for us and set us free from sin. Before we are ever called to be a leader, we are called to be a follower of the LEADER. This forgiveness and grace that we have received have begun a chain reaction in our life under the leading of the Holy Spirit, we are being transformed daily by the renewing of our minds to become more like the image of our Lord and Savior Jesus Christ. As we mature in His likeness and image, we will naturally want to share this message of hope and grace with as many others as possible. The foundation of our ministry must be Jesus Christ.

"The foundation of ministry must be Jesus Christ." - What simple words, why take up space in a book for pastors with them? The reason is that it's incredibly easy to get caught up in the motions of pastoring so much so that you totally forget about the most important relationship in your own life. For some pastors, this has or will, unfortunately, manifest in a variety of terrible, public ways: moral failure, ministry burnout, extreme depression, narcism, or even suicide. For many of the rest of us, we will experience seasons where we may not have had a moral failure or full-blown burnout, but good "churchy" things tend to have a way of getting in the way of the best - Jesus. When we think we can avoid reading the Word and praying personally because we are preparing a sermon - we are headed for trouble. When we think that the Word primarily speaks to "those ignorant people" in our congregations that annoy us, but rarely see the Word correcting us - we are in trouble. When we expect or even demand grace for our sinful actions, but show a level of harshness for the transgressions of others, we are in SERIOUS trouble.

Satan has a way of sneaking into the best of church situations and destroying people who were at one time dedicated fully to the work of the Lord...

> *If you forgive anyone anything, I too forgive that one; and what I have forgiven, if I have forgiven anything, has been for your sakes in the presence [and with the approval] of Christ (the Messiah), To keep Satan from getting the advantage over us; for we are not ignorant of his wiles and intentions. 2 Corinthians 2:10,11 The Amplified Bible*

The Apostle Paul exhorts us in 2 Corinthians 2:11 to forgive people. In verse 12, he explains under the inspiration of the Holy Spirit that it is that forgiveness that "keep(s) Satan from getting the advantage over us; for we are not ignorant of his wiles and intentions." 2 Cor 2:10,11 **The Amplified Bible**

The Amplified Bible translates that the Devil has both "wiles and intentions." Many other translations translate only "schemes." The idea of intention is also something to consider closely, because just as the Master warned Peter that "Satan has asked to sift each of you like wheat" (Luke 22:31 New Living Translation), Satan has "intentions" for every pastor. It is Satan's desire to steal, kill and destroy every Christian (see John 10:10), but as a pastor, if Satan can take you down, he will win a larger victory. When a pastor goes down, even a pastor of a smaller congregation in a church of 30 people, often that pastor and church touches and directly influences 100 or more for the Kingdom of God. How much more damaging for the leader of a church of 100, 200, 1,000 or 3,000 to be taken out of the race by the devil's intentions. Each and every pastor is vital to the Kingdom work, and each pastor is targeted by Satan because of their Kingdom's influence and impact.

For these reasons, it is imperative that as pastors, we stay in daily communion and fellowship with our Lord and Savior. The glamor of the big day at church, the newly built auditorium or the record amount of funds in the offering will always pull at our heartstrings as human beings, but if we are not anchored in who Jesus is and if we are not growing into more of His image daily, we are destined for ministry failure. Ministry failure will not stop at us or our marriage and family, but it will affect every person that we minister to in some way or another. Pastors must keep Jesus at the center of our daily life and routines. We must enter the pulpit and board room knowing we have a clear conscience sprinkled freshly clean again by His precious blood, and we hold no grudge against any. We walk in constant forgiveness through our daily prayer life, and we grant that forgiveness to those around us.

EVERY DAY, the pastor must be in a place of personal prayer, repentance, and Bible Study before the Lord. Before we minister to others, we must meet the Master fresh and new, in the quiet place, ourselves.

1.4 The Cornerstone of the Church

I had the privilege of speaking to Dr. Kevin Drew Robinson, Pastor of Divine Empowerment International Church in Fayetteville, North Carolina. Dr. Robinson leads a church with more than 16 cultures and ethnicities represented. As an African American gentleman, Dr. Robinson leads one of, if not the only, church in Fayetteville, which is a cross-cultural ministry, pastored by an African American leader. We were discussing how the Lord has done many marvelous things in this ministry concerning race over the last 13 years. At the time of this writing, our country is experiencing racial tension that would seem to be at a higher point than at any other time of my almost 45 years of being on the planet. I believe that Dr. Robinson's church may be winning people from many cultures and ethnicities in part because their church is not about race or color, but their church strives to put Jesus first. The church strives to lead people to be Christians first.

While churches may not put race above Christ, many churches and pastors seem to get a lot of things before Christ. It is easy to become known as the church that attracts mainly one thing or another - motorcycle enthusiasts, teachers or those in the educational field, military members, a certain race or ethnicity, people who struggle primarily with recovering from drug or alcohol abuse, the "cool/attractional" church with lights and smoke machines, the church for young professionals, the church for tall people over 6 foot 4 inches tall

(OK, so I haven't seen the last group there). Nothing in and of itself is wrong or evil about a church attracting members with commonalities among them. Surely, many will say that this is natural and cannot even be stopped. The Association of Related Churches, which is possibly the most, numerically successful church planting organization in 2019, even teaches their church planters that to market to everyone, you market to no one. This is based on principles taught by marketing guru, Seth Godin who wrote in his blog…

> **Marketing to nobody**
>
> *Nobody wears a watch any more.*
>
> *Nobody wears a tie either.*
>
> *Nobody shops at a bookstore, at least nobody I know.*
>
> *The market of nobody is big indeed. You can do really well selling to nobody if you do your homework. In fact, most companies selling to nobody outperform those that are trying to sell to everyone.*[2]

There is nothing wrong with certain social groupings if those groups are not exclusive and do not hate or discriminate against groups outside their norm, but it is easy for a church to become so caught up in an activity or cause that this becomes their identity. Many things can take the place of Christ in our hearts. It is not only the affinity groups our churches may be associated with, but it may be the actual process of "church." Many pastor's personal identities become confused with what it should be. Visiting hospitals and calling

---

[2] Godin, Seth, "'Marketing to Nobody", Seth's Blog, May 10, 2011; accessed May 10, 2019, https://seths.blog/2011/05/marketing-to-nobody/

the missing, makes people feel a special tie to us that brings a certain kind of influence and power. This influence and power are not bad in itself, but it must be kept in check when our egos begin to get in the way. If we allow it to run unchecked, the more people, the more power and before too long, we begin to worship this relationship with power and influence rather than Jesus. When this happens, the pastor is in a very bad place and can start to think that this is "my church" when in reality, it all belongs to Jesus. If a pastor lets this go unchecked, what will he do when he is no longer the pastor? Because of this, some pastors can often not let go of a church when it is clearly time to move on.

The churches' identity and the pastor's identity must remain (and the true Church will always have its identity as), "The Bride of Christ."

> **Let us be glad and rejoice and give Him glory, for the marriage of the Lamb has come, and His wife has made herself ready. Revelation 19:7 New King James Version**

Jesus has called us His bride, and the Church is to make ourselves ready for Him. A happy bride is always thinking about that wedding day. They are busy sending out invitations, planning the perfect place for the reception, deciding on what dress to choose with the giggling bridesmaids, and decorating the church to make sure it looks better and fancier than the last wedding that was hosted there. All the preparation is not just for the sake of the big day; the real joy will be when she is united intimately and permanently with the man of her dreams. It is her heart's desire to love and be loved by her husband, and this is no drudgery at all.

Like the happily engaged young lady, looking forward to the big day, we as the Church are to be looking forward to the big day with our Lord. This has to do with our heart's desire. This is not to be a bad, arranged marriage where a set of parents force the bride to get married to someone that she does not know and does not care for. The Churches' love for the bridegroom is to be a love story. The kind of desire that we see described in the Song of Solomon. Our fascination as pastors, church planters and revitalizers, is to be solely in love with Jesus. Our desire is to lead others in a relationship that knows Him personally, intimately, and to know that when we are out of close fellowship with Him, through the power of the Holy Spirit, we are losing something very special indeed. Jesus loves us so much that He gave His life for us. He is jealous for His bride.

> *I am jealous for you with a godly jealousy. I promised you to one husband, to Christ, so that I might present you as a pure virgin to him. 2 Corinthians 11:2* **New International Version**

Have you ever met a person that was so magnetic, had such a great personality, the smile on their face, the words of wisdom, and most especially the joy that exudes from them that you wanted to be around that person as much as possible? This is the way we must see and know Jesus. Time with Jesus always makes us better. Time with Jesus always makes us more giving, grace-filled, kind, considerate, joyful, patient, loving (Seems like there may be a list and name for this stuff in the Bible, doesn't it?). If pastoring, or the local church, ever gets in the way of Jesus being at the heart and the center of our reason for being, we have failed. We may still have a crowd, money, missions programs, a big youth group or influence in the community, but we have failed. It is Jesus that died for us. It is Jesus that set us free. It is Christ that is the chief cornerstone of the Church…

The stone that the builders rejected has now become the cornerstone. Psalms 118:22 **New Living Translation**

A Prayer for Me and You:

O, Lord, keep Christ at the Center of our lives and churches. Let us not put anything before You and Your Kingdom purposes. Father, please help me never to put the growth of the church in front of the heart of the Church - which is Jesus. If church growth, strategies, or fancy programs ever come before my relationship with You, please correct me quickly and gently (if possible), that I might be able to live a life and lead a ministry that is pleasing to You. Help us make disciples that will have life change in this life and will forever know You in eternity.

CHAPTER 2

MODERN SPIRIT FILLED CHURCHES, SPIRIT WARFARE IN CHURCH PLANTING AND MIRACLES

2.1 The Modern Spirit-Filled Church

In today's American climate, many pastors are frightened to claim that they are Spirit-filled or, God forbid, Pentecostal or Charismatic in public settings, on social media or on a church website. Increasingly, America is more and more anti-God in general, anti-Church, and the more one claims to be Evangelically, Bible-believing or Spirit-filled, then the more they can expect push back and negativity from the world. These sentiments discourage churches and pastors from advertising much about what we believe, but it is what we believe that sets us apart from a lifeless, weak watered-down version of Christianity.

> *Having a form of godliness, but denying the power thereof: from such turn away. For of this sort are they which creep into houses, and lead captive silly women*

> *laden with sins, led away with divers lusts, Ever learning, and never able to come to the knowledge of the truth. 2 Timothy 3:5-7* **King James Version (KJV)**

The Word reminds us that we have power in Jesus. We have power to see lives transformed and remade in Jesus' name, but when we deny this power, we have no power at all.

I have felt this pressure in the past as a pastor to not advertise the power we have in Jesus, and I am sure that sometimes I have given into it and at other times, I have taken a hit for being Pentecostal or Charismatic. As I have aged in life and ministry, it has become apparent to me that there is no good reason spiritually or in even the business sense of pastoring and building a church to be concerned a lot with what prospective members think of my theology or the churches' theology. Ultimately, either we believe in and practice the gifts of the Spirit, or we do not.

It is not the Spirit of God that turns people off; it is the excess of people, the goofiness of people and letting the flesh get in the way in church services that turns people off. The Holy Spirit is LIFE. He is the very essence of our perfect creator and Savior, made manifest in our church services and wherever He chooses to reveal Himself in day to day life. It is not the Spirit of God that we should ever be ashamed of, rather, it is the abuse of spiritual gifts and hyper-over spiritually active people that we must be cautious of in church services and fellowship settings.

Recently we were speaking at a service where the pastor was absent. It was made clear at the start of service that the pastor was not present and that I would be the guest speaker for the day. During the praise and worship music, a man loudly interrupted, presumptively to give a "Word from the Lord." While the Word was not necessarily wrong, it was unneeded and added little to nothing to the service. It seemed to turn off the person moderating the service. Later, I went to speak, during my speaking, this same man, loudly interrupted my speaking to interject silly things that were again, not necessarily wrong, but his comments were certainly unnecessary at best. After church, I was introduced to him by a friend, and the friend explained before I met him that he was very, very spiritual, and knew the Bible greatly. In this service setting, after church, we have a table set up where people can get more information about our ministry, give to the ministry, get love gifts or receive more information. Shortly after I went to the table, after their friend's introduction, the man came to the table. He did not cease to speak for some 20 minutes. He shared all kinds of super-spiritual stories and totally monopolized my time. Since we were at a small church with only a few dozen people anyway, I allowed him to talk. He shared minute details of all kinds of spiritual experiences from 20 years in the past that all revolved around his deep spiritual experience.

Later at lunch, I asked the person who was hosting the service that day, who was this man? He explained that even though they had attended the church for more than 18 months, they had never once seen the man before. This man, who did not attend the church, as soon as he heard that the pastor was not present, took it upon himself to publicly give a "Word from the Lord", interrupt the preaching, and monopolize the guest speaker's time at the table. The person hosting us at lunch explained that the man was very arrogant in his presumption to interrupt the service with a "Word" even though no one knew him; he had no permission to do so, and it was his first time attending. I totally agreed. (If I had pastored this church, and this man did this, we would have had a talk very quickly. As a visiting guest, this was not my place.)

Experiences like that are what turn people off from the things of the Lord. I tend to think it was people like this that the Apostle Paul gave much teaching concerning when he said under the inspiration from the Spirit in his call to orderly worship in Corinthians that,

> *"When you meet together, one will sing, another will teach, another will tell some special revelation God has given, one will speak in tongues, and another will interpret what is said. But everything that is done must strengthen all of you."* 1 Corinthians 14:26b **New Living Translation**

> Paul continues, *"If you claim to be a prophet or think you are spiritual, you should recognize that what I am saying is a command from the Lord himself. But if you do not recognize this, you yourself will not be recognized. So, my dear brothers and sisters, be eager to prophesy, and don't forbid speaking in tongues. But be sure that everything is done properly and in order."* 1 Corinthians 14:37-40 **New Living Translation**

It would seem that many churches go to two extremes when it comes to Pentecostal expressions of faith and Charismatic utterances and gifts. On one end of the spectrum, many churches do not allow any gifts to operate outside of the gift of preaching. On the other end of the spectrum, some churches allow ANYTHING and EVERYTHING in the name of Pentecost.

Paul's letters to the Corinthians make it very clear that neither of these views is correct in church services. We are to allow spiritual gifts to operate, but we have a very easy to understand set of guidelines by which we're to abide. (see 1 Corinthians 14 in its entirety)

We will never please all the world when it comes to liking our church. If we do please the world, we are making a grave mistake…

> *You adulterous people! Do you not know that friendship with the world is enmity with God? Therefore whoever wishes to be a friend of the world makes himself an enemy of God. James 4:4* **English Standard Version**

At the end of the day, the Church is to be the Church, and we will never be able to be fully accepted by people who do not know the Lord. There is nothing wrong with theatrical lighting, smoke machines, lots of bass in the sound system, contemporary worship songs, mac computers, red keyboards, skinny jeans and changing our methods with the time, but there is something greatly wrong with excluding the Spirit and welcoming the attitudes of the world. We are called to be a people who are filled with the Spirit of God, and the Spirit of God is not compatible with the Spirit of the land.

We must realize as time passes and we are ever closer to the soon return of the Lord Jesus Christ, that we will not be loved by everybody, and even in America, the Church will be hated more and more if we stand for the truth of the Word of God. At the same time, we are in tremendous company when we are hated by the world...

> *"If the world hates you, keep in mind that it hated me first. If you belonged to the world, it would love you as its own. As it is, you do not belong to the world, but I have chosen you out of the world. That is why the world hates you. John 15:18,19* **New International Version**

While we are hated for Christ's sake all the day long, the world simultaneously will not be able to resist the love and power of Jesus. When the people of God stand for truth in love, we have the ability to win the lost as we unashamedly proclaim that Jesus is Lord, He is the answer to all the world's problems, and He can radically transform your life. It is the power of the Blood of the Lamb and our testimony by which we overcome the world!

> *And I heard a loud voice saying in heaven, Now is come salvation, and strength, and the kingdom of our God, and the power of his Christ: for the accuser of our brethren is cast down, which accused them before our God day and night. And they overcame him by the blood of the Lamb, and by the word of their testimony; and they loved not their lives unto the death. Revelation 12:10,11* **King James Version**

In today's increasingly anti-Church American society, there is nothing wrong whatsoever with being wise among the watching world. The Master reminds us that, *"Look, I am sending you out as sheep among wolves. So be as shrewd as snakes and harmless as doves." Matthew 10:16* **New Living Translation (NLT)** When people are choosing a church, or considering attending one, it is a wonderful thing that we have prepared well for their visit.

I was naturally shy as a child and teenager, and still today as an introvert that God has taught how to act like an extrovert for His purposes, I have an interesting take on attending churches for the first time. I can assure you that if you have been pastoring for a few years, there is a very good chance that you have forgotten how frightening it is to attend a new church. Most of the time, for the last few years, I am speaking in churches that I visit, but from time to time, we have the opportunity to visit churches anonymously. When you step foot on a church property, you have no idea how you will be treated. Often, you are treated poorly with no one speaking to you, no signage as to where the bathrooms are, and a general feeling that you are not really welcomed on the property. It is more like you are being tolerated. When I attend somewhere new as an anonymous guest, I always hate it when my wife goes to the restroom and leaves me in a lobby full of people. In my natural flesh, I would prefer not to speak to anyone. It is an old habit that is hard to break. In those moments, I am reminded that for someone like me, it is totally ridiculous. I am a Christian, a pastor, I have much Christian education, have served in denominational roles and yet, I often feel a little uneasy in new church settings. Even though I'm weird! :) Imagine that if I can feel this way, how many more times does an unsaved person who has not been to church in 20 years or possibly has never been to a church at all feel?

Anything that a church can do in advance to prepare an environment where people feel loved and accepted; this is a good thing. When I was starting out in the ministry years ago, it was often said how important it was that your church facility looks very nice with well-manicured lawns, no trash, and a neat and orderly appearance. While this is, of course, still important, the reason is secondary today. In 1992, it was important that the church look nice because this was the visitors' first impression. Today, this is no longer true. Today, your churches' website must be well polished, modern looking, informative, logical and welcoming. Your website will certainly be the first impression for the vast majority of potential visitors. Your social feeds will be judged as well before anyone ever steps foot on your property. Making the website welcoming, up to date, user-friendly, modern and helpful is a great idea. When the guest arrives at the church property using parking lot greeters, door greeters and lots of happy people will also assist in the process of welcoming new prospects. The idea of welcoming people starts with the website, continues with the parking lot, and permeates everything we do or do not do inside the church building and service. If we only utilize senior adults, we will probably ostracize young families, and if our only music is from decades ago, we may also send the wrong message to a new generation of potential believers.

While we do not have to all be exactly alike, and while every church is not necessarily called to reach the same group of people, we can all at least make an effort to make younger families and youths welcomed in our services. With every generation, style changes, but the message of Jesus does not. Whether we utilize theatrical lighting, modern worship songs, slightly change our vocabulary to better communicate to a new generation or not, these things do not remove the power and presence of the Holy Spirit. We are not compromising the Gospel when we change music styles; we are compromising the Gospel when we become ashamed of the name and power of Jesus and when we allow no place for the gifts of the Spirit in the local church.

Allow the style to change. Allow the new music. Allow the skinny jeans (or whatever the latest style fad may be in five, ten or fifteen years from now), but do not allow friendship with the world by compromising the core message of the Gospel. We are all sinners. Our sin has sentenced us to death. We are incapable of completely freeing ourself from this curse of sin, but praise be to God, Jesus has paid the price for our sin. Jesus has died in my place. Jesus has taken the keys to death, hell, and the grave. Jesus defeated death and rose victoriously from the grave! When I place my faith and trust in Him, sin no longer has a hold on me! Jesus has sent the Holy Spirit to empower me with the very same power that rose Jesus from the grave! Today the Church of Jesus Christ is not powerless but powerful to see miracles, healings, setting people free from the bonds of Satan, tongues, prophecies, and the love that only comes from the Father!

The modern-day Spirit-Filled Church has no reason to hide our power and promise of the precious Holy Spirit. The world is going to hate us anyway, so why not be honest and about who we are in the first place. At the same time, there is nothing wrong with changing our methods and styles to reach as many people as we possibly can. We will never reach everyone, that is just not how it works, but we must strive to reach as many as possible with the good news of Jesus Christ until He returns.

The modern-day Spirit-filled Church may look a little different than we did a few decades ago, we may even sound a little different, but our identity as a Spirit-filled people should never be minimized. The spiritual excesses of people should not have been tolerated years ago, and the spiritual excesses of people should be tolerated no less in modern Spirit-Filled services. If we let people do whatever they want to do in church services with no guidelines, we will quickly have chaos that any sane person would not desire to be included in. In the modern era of American churches, let us be patient and kind to all, practicing grace when someone may occasionally overstep their bounds, but let us also have the courage to set people down who may bring contempt to the Body of Christ.

In the modern-day Spirit-filled church, we can make a place for the supernatural. It is not difficult. It begins with our speech. In many churches that you visit today (even churches that are connected to a Spirit-filled background or denomination), you may never hear a mention of the Holy Spirit. Sometimes churches will never mention demons, healings, pleading the Blood of Jesus, anointing with oil, discerning of spirits, tongues, words of knowledge, words of wisdom and the like. These churches may possibly feel that these things will turn people away from the church. I believe, should God give us this time on the planet before He returns, in the 2020s, 2030s and beyond, people will need and many will desire to hear the entire message of the Gospel more than ever before. As the world becomes more and more blatantly evil, the power of the Cross and the gifts of the Holy Spirit are more needed than ever before. We do not have to frighten people. We do not have to be loud and forceful with our every word, but we can gently, calmly and logically show both the need for the Spirit-Filled experience and a clear demonstration of the Spirit-filled experience.

For me, the Spirit-Filled experience (and the physical manifestation of healing that sometimes accompanies the Spirit-filled life) saved my son's life and for that, I am forever grateful. I am so grateful, that it would be very selfish for me not to share the whole Gospel with people who may also need to experience all that God has for them.

2.2 Opposition and Spiritual Warfare in Church Planting and Church Revitalization

After recently studying some twenty-five books or more on church planting and literally hundreds of articles on the subject for my Doctor of Ministry in Church Planting and Revitalization, some key themes become clear as they stand out over and over again. One of those themes is that if you start a church or make plans to revitalize an old, dying church - THERE WILL BE OPPOSITION. I have read accounts from people in all different tribes of Christianity on the subject, and one of the key themes in church planting material is that once you start this process, there will be expected and often unexpected opposition. Anytime when we are being positioned to move the Kingdom of God forward, there will be an Enemy that will do everything in his (limited) power to stop us.

> *Be sober [well balanced and self-disciplined], be alert and cautious at all times. That enemy of yours, the devil, prowls around like a roaring lion [fiercely hungry], seeking someone to devour. But resist him, be firm in your faith [against his attack—rooted, established, immovable], knowing that the same experiences of*

> *suffering are being experienced by your brothers and sisters throughout the world. [You do not suffer alone.]*
> 1 Peter 5:8,9 **The Amplified Bible**

When people set out to start churches, a conflict has begun that goes to the heart of Satan's plans for this world. Satan tempted Jesus with the kingdoms of this world...

> *And he led Him up and showed Him all the kingdoms of the world in a moment of time. And the devil said to Him, "I will give You all this domain and its glory; for it has been handed over to me, and I give it to whomever I wish. Therefore if You worship before me, it shall all be Yours." Jesus answered him, "It is written, 'You shall worship the Lord your God and serve Him only.'"* Luke 4:5-8 **New American Standard Bible**

While Satan may have some temporary say over the world systems that influence this earth, ultimately, the whole earth is the Lords. When we participate in Kingdom work that rightfully brings people, places and things back into alignment with the Creator of the universe, it understandably upsets Satan. When a church planter sets out to see a community transformed by the power of Jesus or when a church revitalizer decides to take back church territory that has been ceded to Satan over time, all hell breaks loose against this Kingdom advancement.

It is interesting to note that even denominations, churches, and leaders that do not normally talk all that "spiritual" tend to lay that aside when they describe some of the things that occur when their planters started out to plant new works. This is because of the tenacity of Satan and his minions' level of attack against church planters and their families. Joel Rainey describes in his book *Planting Churches in the Real World* how his child began to have seizures, he developed apnea and his marriage was attacked (fighting with each other all the time).[3] Jim Griffith and Bill Easum, in their classic church planting text, *Ten Most Common Mistakes Made by New Church Starts,* list "Failing to Take the Opposition Seriously" as the number two major mistake that church plants and planters make. Griffith and Easum (between the two, this pair has consulted on-site with more than 600 churches and personally started five churches) devoted an entire chapter to opposition.[4]

Church planting opposition comes from every direction. Internally, people in the new church often fight against the new church, churches in the community may rise up against the plant, and even denominations may turn against a new church. People inside the new church plant may turn against the church, often these people have moved from another town where they were committed church members. It is not uncommon for these folks to demand that the new church look and operate exactly like their old church, and if it does not, they will not stay. Sometimes they will attack the new church because it is not the same. Other times, let's face facts, new people in a church plant were basically kicked out of positions in their old church. Sometimes they are trouble makers. These folks are looking for a new church to terrorize. In one of our churches, we had someone working with our presentation computer that I thought possibly had had some difficulties in their last church. After a couple of months, with seemingly no problems, our sound booth computer "lost" all the files connected to Powerpoint that we were using at that time (in the early 2000s) for our songs and sermon points. This

---

[3] Joel Rainey, Church Planting in the Real World (Smyrna, DE: Missional Press, 2008), 123-124.
[4] Jim Griffith and Bill Easum, Ten Most Common Mistakes Made by New Church Starts (St. Louis, MO: Chalice Press, 2008), 13.

seemed strange since the computer was not connected to the internet and no other files had any problems; it was as if the files were simply deleted during church service. We took this in stride and prayerfully and thoughtfully moved on with life. About 3 months later, it happened again with the same person running the computer. They seemed to really like the attention this produced. On the second time, without accusing anyone of anything, we quietly and cordially removed them from their position. This infuriated them, but we moved on with life. Later, this person had several times that they caused problems in the church until we parted ways. A new church plant attracts lots of "interesting" people.

Almost unbelievably, a new church planter who went to plant in a small town reported that he received a call from the four evangelical pastors in his town. When the new pastor went to meet with them, he discovered that they had all decided to meet to explain to him how the town did not need another church.[5] These types of things normally do not produce a long-lasting devastating effect on the new church.

At other times, other churches and leaders from within the same denomination as the new plant may cause very serious issues for the new plant. If the district supervisor or presbyter or whatever the polity may be of the new planter's area supervisor is not on board with the new plant, serious issues may develop. If the person in that position is actively pastoring in the same local area, if they are not a true man or woman of prayer who walks in humility and has a true Kingdom mindset, unfortunately, it is not at all uncommon for them to fight both blatantly and behind the scenes to halt the new work. Church planting books often cite stories of planters who were unexpectedly attacked by their own denomination. While we cannot control other pastors, many church planting veterans suggest that it

---

[5] Griffith and Easum, 14.

is best if before going to a town or city to begin planting that we at least meet with the pastors of the same denomination to share our heart and vision. Possibly, some insecure pastors may be calmed if the information is shared with them that the planter will have no intention to "go after" their people. In reality, many have found that this makes little difference as, no matter how hard the planter tries, he cannot completely control if people choose to come and support their work, even if they go out of their way to not be accommodating to church people from the same denomination (or extremely similar groups). Personally, I have met with the district representatives from the denomination I was working with before I planted to share that I had no intention of trying to take people from their church. Possibly this helped? It is hard to say. I have heard of a planting pastor who moved into an area that had a church from his own denomination. The new church became a very fast-growing congregation that soon numerically surpassed the other churches in the area from the same denomination. He allowed people to attend the new church from the other denominational churches, but he made them wait for three years before they could be in any type of leadership. (Not that this should be a requirement, or that it is a good idea for everyone. This type of guideline should certainly NOT be suggested by other denominational pastors or supervisors in the area.) For this church though, which was the planter's own idea, it seemed to work well.

Another book, *Church Planting Landmines*, shared many other thoughts on Spiritual Warfare and General Opposition. This book lists the following as tools that the Enemy uses against planters: discouragement, sin in the camp, physical hardship, emotional hardship, fear, and derailment.[6]

---

[6] Tom Nebel and Gary Rohrmayer, Church Planting Landmines: Mistakes to Avoid in Years 2 through 10 (Bloomington, MN: Church Smart Resources, 2005), 103-107.

Discouragement

"Criticism, threat, rumor or innuendo" are listed as powerful weapons that Satan uses in the discouragement strategy of church planters.[7] One of the greatest things a church member or fellow minister can do for a church planter is to offer a word of encouragement. Often, church planters have left established positions in healthy and many times large and vibrant churches. When they were in these positions, they often had the ability in the flesh to ward off discouragement attacks because they knew that no matter what anyone said, they walked in a level of "success." When a planter decides to start a new church, there is often nothing that looks remotely like "success" for weeks, months or sometimes even years. When I left the very large church I was working at to start a church twenty years ago, the last service at that church, I preached to one of the churches' smallest Sunday evening crowds of about 400 people, the next time I spoke to a "church" group in our new plant, there were 11 people, all of whom were related to me. Over the next few months, it was amazing to see the things that were said against me. I remember clearly that one person working at a local beauty salon had been told I had had an affair - this was a complete and utter fabrication with no basis whatsoever in reality. Satan will concoct lies and rumors that are designed for the purpose of abortion of the new work. He doesn't need any good reason; he simply is the father of lies. Church planters MUST be in the Word daily, not for sermon preparation, but so they can stay alive in the war for their soul and the soul of the new church.

Sin in the camp

Like the story of Achan in the Bible, one person's sin can often have a devastating effect on the entire fellowship. Stories are told of

---

[7] Nebel and Rohrmayer, 103.

new churches struggling beyond comprehension to have any forward traction, later it was discovered in some cases that people were stealing from new churches' funds, and in another case, the pastor was secretly practicing homosexuality.[8] Sometimes the sin belongs to the planter themselves, and sometimes it can be someone inside the church. We must offer much grace for those who may be caught in sin. In the case of the thief, the pastors were able to gently confront them, take care of the situation, and eventually, the matter was resolved, the person forgiven and even restored to fellowship with the church.

In my own experience, I have seen a new Christian who started making veiled sexual advances at a member of the congregation. Unfortunately, this resulted in the person leaving the group after being lovingly confronted about the situation. A true pastor will often be putting out fires and wisely dispensing church discipline with grace from time to time, but the level and frequency that this occurs in a new plant seems to be greater than in an established church.

Physical Hardship

Young ministers (including myself twenty years ago) often see almost every negative thing that happens as a direct result of Satan's intervention, but more frequently, we are simply living in a fallen world. Shortly after becoming a senior pastor for a few months, I realized that not everything is Satan's fault. Sometimes people die because it is appointed unto man once to die and after this the judgment. Sometimes cars break down because they are not maintained or simply because they have 400,000 miles on the engine. Sometimes we get sick because we have not taken care of ourselves or simply because, with age, the body degrades.

---

[8] Nebel and Rohrmayer, 104.

In church planting, all the regular ills of life are present as they are for everyone, but most everyone that has ever successfully or unsuccessfully attempted to plant a church can tell you that there seems to be an extraordinary amount of physical attack. Gary Rohrmayer tells the story of his wife getting strep throat six times in less than six months while they were planting a church. The situation had gotten so severe that they were planning to have surgery to stop the infections. While they were praying about the situation, they received a letter from a missionary friend on a Wednesday before a church service. In the letter, the missionary "coincidentally" explained how his wife had had strep throat five times. From this, the planter was aware that this was a special attack from the enemy. That evening in the mid-week service, he asked the church to agree and fervently pray with him for a complete and special healing of his wife's ailment. She started to feel better immediately. After going to the doctor to prepare for the surgery, the doctor said that the surgery was only needed if she really wanted it because her throat was "one hundred times better." She never had the surgery and never again had strep throat.[9]

Another story is told of a church-planting pastor that had their washing machine, dryer, lawnmower and both of their cars all die in two weeks.[10] Situations like this could happen to anyone at any time, but when it happens to a church planter who has given their all to be in the heat of it for the Kingdom, you really have to wonder. In my own life, during successful and unsuccessful church planting attempts, we have seen what would seem to be the direct influence of Satan. Some of these times, I passed the test, and other times I failed. What cannot be denied is that during seasons of church planting, great opposition is to be expected, but the help of an even greater God is also to be expected…

---

[9] Nebel and Rohrmayer, 105.
[10] Nebel and Rohrmayer, 105.

> *"But every spirit that does not acknowledge Jesus is not from God. This is the spirit of the antichrist, which you have heard is coming and even now is already in the world. You, dear children, are from God and have overcome them, because the one who is in you is greater than the one who is in the world."* **1 John 4:4 NIV**

In church planting, a pastor cannot only count on strong opposition from the Enemy and even stronger help from the Lord of Hosts; the pastor may sometimes experience full-blown miracles.

2.3 The Place of Miracles in Church Planting

When someone steps out on faith in order for God to touch a city, change a region, impact the nation or touch the world, these types of spiritual endeavors are especially hated by the prince of the power of the air. The devil will launch his greatest attack against the child of God and the future church. In response, God always provides help and assistance, but at times, God does something very special. At times, God does extraordinary miracles, which sets the new church up for success and long term viability.

In the year 2000, we saw God do one of those special things. After landing in Pensacola, Florida, to establish a church in early June of that year, we began to be concerned with the behavior of our youngest son. By November of 2000, the group of 11 people had grown to about 45-55, and we were very excited about what God was doing at the fledgling new congregation. Simultaneously, our baby son's behavior was increasingly strange. Andrew Micah Farley, who was now about 16 months old, had become extremely difficult to control. Andrew had an older brother, and we believed in the proper, loving, careful correction of your children. We never disciplined them in anger, but we did discipline them. Andrew, though, seemed to have never-ending energy. At this point in my life, I had been a youth pastor for almost a decade at large and mega-churches. I had seen a lot of children and teens with attention deficit disorder, hyperactivity syndromes and the like, but my baby son seemed to have far more energy than any other child we had ever encountered.

Increasingly, we noticed that not only did Andrew have an unbelievable amount of energy, but he was exceedingly strong at times. Andrew reminded us of "BamBam" from the old Flintstones cartoon. This child would hardly sleep at night, and you could not keep up with him. At the time, as parents, we were both 26 years old and in relatively good shape. When Andrew would get into certain moods, it physically was not possible for me to contain or control him. Keep in mind, Andrew was a baby, sixteen-month-old boy of regular size, but when he would get disobedient or mad, I could not physically contain him. As hard as this is to understand, his 16-month-old arms would often be stronger than my 26-year-old arms (that worked several days a week stocking heavy cases and loading and unloading shelves at Walmart when I was not preaching. [I was in great physical shape]). At times, the nursery workers at church could also not contain Andrew; he had a drive and physical energy that was not normal. When he decided he was going to break out of a nursery door, he would. He did so several times during the middle of church services, with none of the nursery workers being able to control or contain him.

After a few months of this behavior, as parents, we began to wonder if something was seriously wrong. While we always prayed for both of our children, we started to intensely pray about what might be the situation with Andrew. We even eventually started considering taking him to the doctor. Many times, he would only sleep a very few hours at night (at age 16 months, not at a month or two old). We were getting little sleep and little peace about the child. It is difficult to explain the power he had and harder still for people reading this account to comprehend the level we are speaking of here, so the next story, which is not an exaggeration, kind of lets you understand what we were dealing with as touching Andrew.

In November of 2000, we had started to pray about taking Andrew to the doctor about these concerns. One day, as normal, we were having a difficult time controlling him. We were walking up the steps to our porch when we had just been talking and praying about how concerned we were for him. We were discussing whether we should consider taking him to the doctor. At this time, we had just moved to the Pensacola area a few months earlier in order to start the church. With limited funds, we had rented a double-wide trailer that was in the back of a lady's yard. The trailer did not have a garage or shed of any kind, only a large, covered front porch. The porch was the only place to store any type of tools, so we kept our lawnmower on the porch. We owned a 6.5 horsepower gasoline-powered push mower. This mower was relatively heavy and was somewhat difficult for me as a strong, 26-year-old man in good shape to get on and off the porch.

As we were getting ready to walk inside the house, Andrew leaned over and grabbed the lawnmower with one hand. In the next second, he picked it up, raising two wheels off the ground. I remember thinking, "This is crazy." As I was watching him, (I would probably not believe this if I had not seen it with my own eyes - [this true story will make more sense as you continue to read]) he continued to lift the mower and with one hand he lifted it completely (all four wheels off the ground) and threw it a few inches across the porch. Right then and there, we knew that something had to be very different, if not very wrong, and we made an appointment to see the doctor right away.[11]

When we arrived at the doctor with Andrew, after getting checked in, he received very speedy care. Once they checked his vitals, they discovered his heart rate was 200 beats per minute, and his blood pressure was also very high. Upon further examination, the physician told us to take him immediately to Sacred Heart Hospital (a large, regional medical facility in Pensacola) to run more tests. Over the next few days, our lives would be turned completely upside down by the results.

In a matter of hours, it was discovered that Andrew had some type of large mass in his abdomen. The doctors were not sure what it was, but they did not think it was anything good, to say the least. Surgery, with a team of specialists, was scheduled and we were told that they expected it to be an extensive operation. When the day came to perform the operation (just a couple of days later), most of the new church members were in the waiting room. Surgery started first thing in the morning and continued until the early evening. Every few hours, a different doctor or surgical team member would come give us an update. This day, a team of several surgeons removed Andrew's right adrenal gland, seven lymph nodes, part of his back muscles, part of a kidney, a portion of the plumbing to that kidney, and a part of his liver. Eventually, the surgery was over, and for now, Andrew was alive. He was strapped down in an infant bed with more tubes and monitors going into and attached to his body than a parent should ever have to see. We were told that for several days, he was one of, if not the most critical patient in the entire hospital.

---

[11] As I typed this page, I quickly looked up the shipping weight of a 6.5 horsepower lawnmower on amazon.com, it showed 80 pounds. So let's assume the mower on the porch that day was somewhere in that weight range. At this time, Andrew weighed approximately 24-26 pounds.

A day or two after the surgery, it eventually became somewhat clear that the baby was moving toward a more stable but still very serious condition, and hopefully, he would live. A meeting was scheduled with the pediatric oncologist (cancer doctor), and those are meetings that you never wish on your worst enemy. At the meeting, the doctor had some answers and some news for us. The doctor explained that the surgeons removed the right adrenal gland because Andrew had one of the rarest cancers known to man, an Adrenocortical carcinoma. He explained that the cancer developed into a functioning tumor. Unlike many cancer tumors, which may eventually take the patient's life by growing and pressing into the vital organ and eventually stopping the functioning of a vital organ like the heart, lungs or kidneys - the "functioning tumor" or "living tumor," takes over the organ. In this case, the tumor took over the right adrenal gland and caused it to produce adrenaline at an accelerated rate. In Andrew's case, it mimicked the fight or flight response. The fight or flight response is the correct and natural condition of the human body (and some animals) whereby the adrenal glands produce and output large amounts of adrenaline when they are threatened. This has been used to describe more than one instance, for example, of small framed grandmothers temporarily having the strength to pick up a car when it had fallen on their grandchild. When the body is in the fight or flight response mode, a variety of hormones work together in an almost super-human way in order to allow the person to flee or fight the threat.

As it was described to us, in Andrew's case and the cases of many other children with this cancer, this can cause the child to have phenomenal energy and strength. This explained the off the charts heart rate, blood pressure, and other vital signs. This was why he had been increasingly difficult to control over the last few months. This was also what killed the vast majority of the people with this disease. At the time of this writing in 2019, several websites say that there is about one Adrenocortical carcinoma per two million people. This is still a very rare cancer. In the year 2000, though, we were told that there were only 33 other documented cases in the world, and 32 of them were dead. Interestingly, the vast majority of these cases were also in children, less than five years old and they were almost all from the city of Manchester, England. (We had never visited England.)

As soon as the physician finished explaining what the cancer was, he immediately went into his next thought. He said, "There is no treatment for this cancer with the exception of removing it. Chemotherapy and radiation make no difference. We took out seven lymph nodes; four were eaten up with cancer, so we know the cancer has spread. We will do further tests, but we know the cancer is also in his brain, bones, and blood. We did the surgery just to extend his life some, but take him home and enjoy him because he will be dead in less than six months."

The Gospels record versions of an account three times when Jesus was telling the disciples not to worry about what to say when they would be placed before magistrates and government officials when they would get arrested in the future (*Matthew 10:19, Mark 13:11 and Luke 12:11*). Depending on the translation, Jesus is saying either that the Holy Spirit would give you the words to say at that time, or in other words, that it would kind of be the Holy Spirit actually speaking through you. (In Spirit-filled Christianity, much is said about "yielding" to the Holy Spirit to say what He wants to say through you while speaking in tongues. I have found that even more frequently, He wants to speak things through me in English that may not make a lot of logical sense, but His logic and power are higher than anything a man can come up with!) I believe the words of Christ concerning the Holy Spirit speaking through us are not confined only to when we get arrested for His cause. There are many times the Spirit will speak through us if we will allow Him and get out of His way. Fortunately, that day, in the cancer doctor's office, was one of those days. As my wife cried her eyes out (it was almost as if someone else was speaking through me), I looked at that doctor and said, "Sir, the Lord is going to heal my son!"

The doctor immediately said, "Listen, I see this all the time, you are in denial, but there is no doubt, unfortunately, your son will die in no more than six months." As if I was speaking a different language and he did not understand the first time, I looked at him again, and I believe the Spirit spoke again, "The Lord is going to heal my son!" At this, the doctor seemed very agitated. He then spoke with all the authority he could muster from behind his M.D. name tag and white physician's coat. He explained that he had been doing this for longer than we had been alive and that there was no doubt that the boy would surely die. He now was showing obvious disdain for me and my behavior. He went on to explain that they would be doing some more tests to verify that the cancer had spread to his brain, bones and blood, but that there was no chance that this had not happened - on all three counts. He continued that the tumor was not only spewing the cancer all through the body via the endocrine system but also explained that the tumor had ripped the adrenal gland apart in the abdomen. The tumor was torn open and leaking cancer into the abdominal cavity. In addition to the cancer being transported all through the body by way of the adrenal gland and being spilled into the abdomen, he also enlightened us that the four lymph nodes that were eaten up with the cancer were also further indication that the cancer was everywhere, already. At this, instead of getting into a full-blown fight with the man, I simply said in a little calmer voice, something to the effect of, "I understand, but you are going to see the Glory of the Lord. He is going to heal my son."

Over the next few days, we waited with great anticipation for the results of a test that had to be sent to California for the results. Finally, we were called back into the cancer doctor's office. The doctor immediately started his speech with, "Do not get excited about what I am going to say." Then he continued, "The tests came back showing no more signs of cancer, but this is impossible. Without a doubt, the cancer is also in his brain, bones and blood. I am positive that the tests results were somehow wrong or tainted, so I am going to send it back for another look. Do not get excited because the results are definitely a fluke. The cancer has certainly spread to his brain, bones and blood."

At this, I looked at the doctor and again said, "Sir, I told you that the Lord was going to heal my son." The physician seemed more irritated with me than he ever had, and said that he was going to send for more test results as this was simply not possible. Another long week passed, and we were called back in to the office. This time, the doctor explained again that there was no sign of cancer, but he assured us that there was some type of catastrophic mistake with the testing and that someone in the testing laboratory very much needed to be fired. I once again reminded the doctor that, "The Lord was going to heal my son." After a third round of tests, that also showed no more cancer; the cancer doctor eventually quit sending it off. As if this was clearly not enough proof that the Lord had either started or completed a work in Andrew, the physician was certain to explain to us that while these tests possibly were somehow correct, that over the next few weeks, CT scans and MRIs would confirm that the cancer would quickly return with a vengeance.

In very short order, our son began to be ran through large, radiated tubes on a regular basis. At first, every few weeks, he would have either a CT or MRI scan. These became so frequent, that the technicians and nurses who were responsible for his care during these procedures began to know Andrew and us on a first-name basis. Eventually, one of the sedation nurses would start attending our church from time to time. In the weeks after the surgery and the initial post-surgery testing, Andrew was submitted to several scans. Each time, we would be required to go see the cancer doctor again. Our visits became adversarial as he had a contempt for me, and I equally had a disdain for him. Each time, the doctor would assure us that the cancer would return. While I am sure he was a fine, dedicated, and disciplined man and physician, I believe that in this situation, it was not actually my spirit that was speaking through me, but it was often, the Holy Spirit Himself speaking through me. (I am reluctant to even write such a claim and make such rarely, but I have no other explanation for the Words I shared, the boldness that was exhibited, and the results that came to pass. All Glory goes to Jesus!) On the other side of these visits, I do not believe that the physician's spirit was speaking either, rather another spirit speaking through him. I am not anti-medicine or anti-science; we appreciate God-given physicians and all the help that a wonderful physician can bring to a hurting individual with the miracles of modern medicine. I can imagine that decades of seeing children die in your practice would harden a man and cause them to believe that there is almost never a chance for supernatural intervention. BUT GOD…sometimes does step in and changes prescribed outcomes and alters the future of people, families, churches, towns, cities, regions, and nations! *"Jesus looked at them and said, 'With man this is impossible, but with God all things are possible.'" **Matthew 19:26 NIV***

Eventually, after the surgery, weeks passed, then a month, then months, then we hit the dreaded six-month time frame - that was the "guaranteed" time of death. Six months, came and went. Nine months, a year, 18 months, all came and passed, each with the reassurance from the doctor that the cancer would surely return.

Somewhere between the two-three year time frame, a scan showed something strange. Immediately, all medical personnel knew that this was the cancer, finally back. The news hit us like a ton of bricks. "Something" was in the pictures of the lungs. At this, I told Heather, "We are not going to tell anyone about this. They will not have the faith to believe for it." When the cancer was first discovered, thousands of people in area churches and from across the country were recruited to pray for Andrew. They were told that a baby boy of a young church planter had been given no hope to live after they had been given the diagnosis of a terminal cancer. This time, I did not believe people who were familiar with the situation would be (for the most part) able to have the faith that this cancer was gone.

For about two weeks, we fought Satan in the battlefield of the mind as he assured us that the doctor was finally right and vindicated - this cancer had come back! This time, it was only my wife and I that knew, we did not even tell our closest family or church friends. I knew that if this time, this battle was this incredibly difficult for the parents to fight, how much more would it be for people who were not as invested in the situation. Fortunately, we were almost full-time at the church by then, and we were able to concentrate on our thinking, daily devotions, prayer and fasting as our primary occupation. Finally, some two weeks later, after more tests, it was determined that this was not a new tumor or tumors, but it was scarring from pneumonia or some type of previous lung infection. By the grace of God, the boy still did not have cancer. This type of scare happened on another occasion, but each time, God was more than faithful.

As time passed by, we grew accustomed to hospital visits, doctors visits, and the continual scans. Eventually, the months turned into years. About four years into the process with Andrew, the initial cancer doctor, died of cancer himself. I offered to pray for him while he was sick, but he refused to let me pray for him. The years stretched out to make a decade, and after ten years we were told by a new cancer doctor that, "I am not saying he is in remission from this cancer because you do not go into remission from this cancer. I will say, if he dies of cancer, it will not be from this cancer."

Over 40 days in the hospital initially, over one million dollars of the initial surgery and treatment, a multiple of countless doctor visits to general practitioners, cancer doctors, endocrine specialists, kidney specialists, MRIs, CT Scans and varying tests- and eventually we were told he was going to live. During that time, the Nemours Children's Clinic chose Andrew as one of their cases of the year to highlight in their Nemours Children's Clinic Annual Report. To give an idea of how rare this cancer is, in the same report where Andrew was featured, there were a total of some four to seven cases highlighted for the entire year. Two of the other cases featured were a child who had to live in a bubble because he had no immune system and another child that was allergic to sunlight. Because, at least in part, to the extreme rarity of the condition, Andrew's medical bills were picked up by the Nemour's Children's Clinics and the Children's Miracle Network. (To this day, we often give a small donation when various retailers ask for a donation to the Children's Miracle Network). We are very thankful for the Nemours Children's Clinic and the Children's Miracle Network.

Amazingly, the healing of this dreaded cancer was not the end to Andrew's healing. After the initial shock of the surgery settled down, we started seeing all these other physicians in the Nemours Children's Clinic. The endocrine specialist and kidney specialist both started to explain that if by some chance, Andrew lived through the cancer, he would need specialized care for his kidney and the hormones in his body. The kidney specialist did explain that from time to time, the kidneys of such a young child may spontaneously re-grow the missing part and the "plumbing" to the kidney. The kidney that had a portion removed and the "plumbing" to that kidney completely healed itself over the next few months and years. (This cannot be called miraculous, as it does naturally occur sometimes, but we give credit and glory to God for this blessing none the less!) The hormone specialist explained that with the complete removal of the right adrenal gland, he would probably also need to have hormone therapy to enter puberty when the time came. Interestingly enough, when Andrew reached puberty (alive and well), he went into puberty naturally and normally with no help from modern medicine. In these ways, God proved Himself to be able to heal completely and totally and supply every need for and through His people. We would have been fine to have had some medical and financial complications with Andrew as long as he was alive. Our good God took care of all the medical bills (even though at this time we had no health insurance), and even healed all the auxiliary medical conditions (which are serious enough in their own right). At the time of this writing, Andrew is 20 years old and has little to no known complications from this entire ordeal.

2.4 The result of this experience- Opposition leads to Victory

From this experience of extreme, spiritual attack which ended in triumphant victory over this Satanic scheme, much was learned. During the times of spiritual attack and struggle that we all go through (and during the amplified times of attack when starting a church), we learn to lean heavily on the Almighty. Often, when everything is going well, people seem to forget to pray and seek the face of God, but when your son's life is on the line, you tend to get closer to God than ever before. Before my son was diagnosed with an "incurable" cancer, I knew from head knowledge that God could heal from all kinds of diseases. Jesus healed in the Gospel accounts, and I had heard of healings in my lifetime. I had been privileged to sit under the teaching of R.W. Schambach while a child at Pace Assembly of God in Pace, Florida. I had heard of great men of God who were used by the Holy Spirit to heal various diseases. In my own family, I heard my grandmother, Edith Demarcus, testify to the Lord's healing power in church services and other family stories. I "knew" that God's miraculous healing was real, but I only "knew" it in my life personally in the form of healing a broken foot.

When Heather and I were first married (at the age of 18), we were young kids, working hard at several jobs and going to college, but we had no health insurance or benefits of any kind. During this time, I was playing basketball with some kids from the church, and as I turned on the court, there was a loud, audible snap sound. I fell to the ground and was immediately in considerable pain. Within a few hours, my ankle was very swollen. We knew a nurse who looked at it. She said she was almost certain that it was broken, and that I would need to go to the emergency room. Instead, that night, we fervently prayed. The next morning when I got up, my leg, foot, and ankle all seemed fine. I went to work as usual that day, and that was the end of it. I am pretty sure; the Lord healed me of a broken ankle or foot.

If you are thinking this story sounds, a little less dynamic, exciting, and dramatic than the story of Andrew's healing of cancer, you would be correct. That is the point. Until this time of opposition, walking through the trial with the Holy Spirit and the ultimate, obvious, and miraculous healing of our son, my "greatest healing testimony" was the equally true and yet simultaneously unimpressive story of the healing of a possibly broken foot. There was no documentation, no doctors visit, none of that. To me, I know that God healed me of what the problem was and at the time, it was pretty serious, we drastically needed every penny we earned from work to make sure we had enough to eat. To us, it was a miracle from God, and to this day, I give Him glory for that.

In this season of life, we travel the country preaching in churches of all sizes, and often, we share Andrew's story of healing. Can you imagine, if the greatest healing story we had was that, we think, we're pretty sure - I broke my foot or ankle, and God healed it. Most likely, I would not be traveling the country testifying to God's amazing, healing power. I would know personally that God could heal a broken foot or ankle, but there is a pretty good chance that no one would have me in their churches to tell such a story.

You see, major, spiritual opposition that is handled correctly can lead to a great victory. **Spiritual opposition can lead to great Victory!** Most every church planting book discusses spiritual opposition. Most every church planting author, warns of the opposition and how we should never underestimate it. This is very true! We should never underestimate the opposition, and we should enlist as many prayer partners as possible to intercede on ours and the future churches' behalf. Surely, most church planting books, make the assumption that we know, we can be victorious over the opposition. We are enabled and equipped to fight the opposition, and we are more than conquerors through Christ Jesus. We have the ability to destroy the works of the Devil, but I want to make it very clear, opposition comes from Satan as an attempt to destroy and derail us and the work of the Church. Allowing opposition is also a way in which God tests us to strengthen us and make us better prepared for His Kingdom service (see the biblical account of Job). How we deal with spiritual opposition causes us to learn much about ourselves, our relationship with God and it even sometimes teaches us about the very nature and character of our awesome God!

In the battle that was fought for Andrew's life, we learned much better on how to depend on God. Times of extreme personal crisis teaches the child of God many things. For me, I was reminded, not to be arrogant, not to judge others, not to take life for granted, not to take health for granted, not to neglect daily spiritual disciplines, and you can trust the Lord 110% with your life, ministry, family and future. During the early months of Andrew's battle with cancer, I found myself praying like never before, walking in levels of discipline I had never known, and searching the scriptures about healing with a totally new hunger for insight and inspiration from the Word of God. As time progressed, it started to become obvious that Andrew was going to pass the six-month mark, and I began to gain a new confidence in the Lord's healing ability. Soon my preaching was filled with themes of Spiritual Warfare and Divine Healing. Before long, others in the church would develop new levels of faith about healing. Over the next 4-5 years, we saw God miraculously heal many people of other "incurable" cancers, some tumors simply vanished as we prayed for them, physicians called several medical observations "miracles" and a baby that had died in the womb (and a D&C was already scheduled to remove the dead fetus) was restored, the D&C was cancelled and that "dead" baby is now almost 20 years old and as healthy as can be. God took what seemed like a massive negative and turned it into something marvelous. From what I learned from the experience and from what the Lord supernaturally imparted to me during that journey, a small revival of sorts of healings was birthed, and many were healed of large, significant physical issues. From these experiences, the faith of many people in the Cantonment, Florida area was greatly strengthened, and over the course of the next few years, 258 people would be baptized in water, several church buildings would be built, and a church planter's dream would become a reality. As Joseph said,

> *"As for you, you meant evil against me, but God meant it for good in order to bring about this present result,*

> *to preserve many people alive."* **Genesis 50:20 New American Standard Bible**

WHAT SATAN, HIS FORCES AND EVEN PEOPLE DO TO ATTACK, HINDER AND TRY TO DESTROY NEW CHURCHES, OFTEN GOD TURNS AROUND AND USES THE MIRACULOUSLY FOR HIS GLORY!

The opposition to your new church will probably be very great, but remember the Lord is greater than any opposition. Satan uses all his spiritual abilities to attack new churches, but God frequently uses miracles (of every kind) to show His Glory in the earth and in the lives of people. As Spirit-filled church planters, let's expect God to move in the miraculous through us and for us as we expand His Kingdom...

> *"Fellow Israelites, listen to this: Jesus of Nazareth was a man accredited by God to you by miracles, wonders and signs, which God did among you through him, as you yourselves know.* **Acts 2:22 New International Version**

Jesus was accredited for miracles, and we can expect that as His servants, doing His will, He will also perform great and mighty works through us.

During the time of Andrew's healing, we attended a church conference when a new praise and worship song was just becoming popular. The song was Terry MacAlmon's, *"You Deserve the Glory."* The song goes...

> *You deserve the glory and the honor.*
> *Lord, we lift our hands in worship,*

As we lift your holy name.

For you are great, You do miracles so great.
There is no one else like you; there is no one else like You.
For you are great, You do miracles so great.
There is no one else like you; there is no one else like You.

Since the song was so popular at that time, it is still used in worship sets from time to time. When I hear those words, I am immediately taken back to Andrew's healing. I am reminded that there is NOTHING that our God cannot do! Whenever you start a church, know that there will be times of testing and opposition, but God will also show Himself faithful. Expect the miraculous.

Over the course of the first few years of our churches' existence, I made many mistakes, there were many ways that people could legitimately criticize this young, brash church planter, but there was little question that God was doing something supernatural at Harvest Christian Center, Cantonment, Florida. At that time, I would certainly have not chosen to go through that trial, if I had been given a choice. In time though, the trial served a greater purpose, and we saw God heal, save, deliver and call many people into ministry. He used Andrew's healing to solidify a church. Whatever God does in the early years of a church plant, we can trust that it will turn out for His glory and our good. We can trust Him with our very lives and be sure that He loves us more than we can imagine.

> "And we know that all things work together for good to them that love God, to them who are called according to his purpose." **Romans 8:28 King James Version**

Whatever a church planter may go through, if they will trust God with the trial, their life, and His church, Jesus will do something glorious with it.

CHAPTER 3

GETTING DOWN TO BUSINESS LEGALLY AND PRACTICALLY

3.1 The Business Side of Church Planting - Legal and Financial Considerations

When starting a new church someone must consider the legal and business ramifications of working in the United States of America (or whatever country in which they do business). While each state has its own specific laws and guidelines for how a church is to legally operate, we must find out what these rules are. When they do not conflict with the Bible, we must abide by them. Some government interference is certainly just that, interference, but many of the laws and guidelines for churches (at least in the United States) are not intended to harm the church. Actually, many states offer special benefits for churches to include exemption from property tax, exemption from local sales taxes, and other benefits. If the initial steps are not taken with attention to detail to be certain that the church is set up correctly, then many of these benefits may not apply.

When we were first getting our church off the ground in Florida, about three months into the process, we had the opportunity to rent an existing church building. It was quickly made known to us that the building was also available for sale as well. After a quick meeting, our new congregation decided that we were interested in purchasing the little church. We had the finances and desire to do so. It would have been no problem for the people attending, and those in leadership would have done whatever was necessary to purchase it.

The realtor was informed that we were interested in buying, and a contract was drawn up. The seller was contacted, and they accepted our offer. Like most real estate transactions, we expected it to take a few weeks to possibly a couple of months to close. We discovered a different reality. When the former church that had occupied the building formed (some 40-60 years earlier), they had never formed a corporation, officially pursued tax-exempt status, written articles of incorporation, or bylaws. This church had existed for more than half a century, and at times, more than 50 people attended the group. During the entire life of the existing church, it had never legally existed as a church in the eyes of the state of Florida. Florida, like many other states, is funny about what happens to the proceeds of a church building when it is sold. (Some pastors have been known to sell a building that they never built, they did not establish the local congregation, their money did not hire people to build it, they never put a nail in a board of the building, and they did not even have the vision to grow the congregation - but they sold the building and collected all the money for it personally.)

So when this "church" (it may have been a church in God's eyes, but it never existed in the county, state, or government's eyes) decided it was time to sell, there was no way to sell it. The last pastor had to go through a lot of hoops. It was required by the state that every person that was or had ever been a member be tracked down. This was interesting. The group spent the next several months taking pictures of gravesites around the area, tracking down death certificates, and eventually finding a handful of former members that had once attended. While I cannot remember the specifics now, some almost twenty years later, they were either required to get permission from each and every living member to sell, or it may have been that the money had to be split amongst the former members. What I can remember is that it was a massive fiasco for them. We ended up moving about ten months later and assimilating another existing church into our fellowship as we took control of their building. In this process, the former church we had rented from lost the sell. For us, it was a blessing, and we never felt like God had wanted us to stay at that property long term, but for the former church, since they had never taken care of business in the entirety of their church life, someone had to take care of business in the churches' death. This lack of business acumen may have inadvertently put all donations to this church in jeopardy of not being tax-deductible. Hopefully, all the givers are now gone on to glory anyway, and no one would ever pursue that, but why put your members and adherents at risk of breaking the tax laws because of the churches' negligence.

This was an extreme example of sloppiness in church business and administration, but unfortunately, many very small churches show little concern for proper business management. Pastors (even very good and gifted pastors) do not feel called or drawn to administrative duties. There is nothing wrong with this. The Bible makes it clear that the primary calling of the fivefold ministries is to equip believers for the work of the ministry.

> *And He gave some as apostles, and some as prophets, and some as evangelists, and some as pastors and teachers, for the equipping of the saints for the work*

of service, to the building up of the body of Christ;
Ephesians 4:11,12 New American Standard Bible

While it is understandable that a pastor may have little desire or skill to do the administrative functions, they are Biblically mandated to equip others to perform ministry service work for the building up of the Kingdom and the local church. One area that church members can excel in is administration. As a pastor, if you are not called and talented to administer business, that's OK, but make sure you find someone or several people who can. When starting a new church, there are several things that need to be in place.

Some of the things that are needed when starting a new church include: employer identification number, articles of incorporation, constitution and bylaws, IRS tax-exempt determination letter, bank accounts, and if they so apply, sales tax exemption certificates and written denominational and/or organizational agreements and understandings. These basic documents are among the minimum requirements to officially and legally begin a church.

Many companies exist that can do these things for you if you have the funding to do so. It is highly recommended that unless the pastor is also an attorney, that all churches employ the professional services of others for these initial documents. It will be well worth the money and the peace of mind to know that these documents are prepared correctly. Some churches will, unfortunately, avoid these proper procedural necessities because they require some work and/or money. The churches which choose to neglect these things have a high probability of regretting this later when problems arise. Also, business people respect proper business, so if you want to attract high level achievers, entrepreneurs and business leaders to your councils, boards, and varying levels of leadership, it is unlikely that they will come if the house is not in order. Most of the things listed can be accomplished by the average person without financial cost by putting some time into them. The one above mentioned item that is more complicated than the others is the IRS Tax determination letter. Whether a church chooses to embark on completing these steps themselves or hiring firms and professionals to assist with the process, the church should see to it that these steps are taken care of early on.

Employer Identification Number or EIN- the EIN is very simple and straight forward to obtain by calling the IRS. It just takes a few minutes on the phone, and anyone can do this. This number serves as the business identification number for the church, serving in the place of a social security number for an individual. It will be used thousands of times over the life of the church. When calling to get the number from the IRS, be sure to be ready to safeguard the number and keep a copy of a form they will email you. This will be required at a minimum to secure bank accounts.

Articles of Incorporation, Constitution, and Bylaws - these documents will put forth the reason for the organization, how it legally operates its organizational governance and the specifics of how people vote, who votes, and things such as this. These documents may take a little time to be developed over the course of several meetings. While you may choose to hire outside assistance to develop these documents, and while you may use a template of another existing church to complete them, it is highly recommended that the planting pastor remain very hands-on in this process. It will be to your advantage to carefully read, participate in the wording and understand every single word that these documents contain. If there is ever a legal challenge to the church in the future, what is written in these documents will prevail. Things like how the pastor is appointed and under what circumstances they may be removed will be a part of these documents. If your church is denominationally affiliated, there may also be requirements from the denomination of specific clauses that are required in these documents. For example, many denominations require that if the local congregation ceases to exist that real estate goes back to the denomination, and not to a pastor or individual. (This may sound controlling, but if you become an Internal Revenue Service 501c3 Tax Exempt Church [as you should], these documents will contain a clause anyway that makes it plain that the organization does not exist to benefit any one individual and if the church closes the real estate will need to be given to another similar organization). If one is getting into the church business with the thought of eventually selling the church building to profit from it personally, you are in it for seriously wrong reasons anyway. While the denominational requirements may seem stifling, there are also normally good protections built into those existing systems that can protect both the pastor and church legally in a variety of situations. It is a great idea to look at several churches founding documents when you are in this process. Rather a church and pastor chooses to outsource some of the work of the articles, bylaws, and constitution or do it completely themselves; make sure that you understand what is being done with this step. Be detail-oriented in reading, crafting and finalizing these documents with much prayer, care, and consideration for the future.

Incorporating the Church and Possible Sales Tax Exemption - Once the church has the founding documents in order, it is possible to incorporate. This process may be different from state to state. It will probably involve sending these documents into your state government to the secretary of state and paying a filing fee. In some states, if there are problems with incorporation paperwork, the state will explain the error. Then the church will simply correct the problem as needed and resubmit. Once the paperwork meets local requirements and the necessary fees are paid, the church will then be incorporated. These steps will help protect the pastor and church leaders legally, spell out how things are done in your local fellowship and also make it possible for the church to perform many business operations such as acquiring a credit card in the churches' name for business purchases and even to eventually purchase land or buildings.

In Florida (where the author is familiar with laws - although they can change frequently), it is possible for a church to become a corporation with these documents and also to acquire Florida sales tax exemption. This means that churches in Florida (and several other states) will not have to pay sales tax on almost any equipment they purchase once these documents are in order. This is a powerful and almost immediately available benefit that should obviously not be ignored. In Florida, once the incorporation paperwork is complete and the church is incorporated, it is a simple process to become sales tax exempt. This exemption lasts about five years and is easy to re-apply for at that time.

IRS Tax Exempt Determination Letter - Your IRS tax determination letter is a letter from the government proving that you are a 501c3 Tax Exempt Organization. This document insures donors and potential donors that their contributions are tax-deductible. Many people will say that this is "automatic" because you are a church. This is not completely true. If the church does not meet very specific requirements, then the church is NOT a tax-deductible 501c3 organization. Of the initial documents which need to be crafted by churches, this is usually the most complex. For this reason, when Brian Farley Ministries Incorporated was setting things up to expand our ministry, we did hire an outside accounting firm that specializes in 501c3s to help us with this. The form to fill out for 501c3 status is over 40 pages long. It is frequently rejected by the IRS and returned to the church or organization requesting 501c3 status if it is not filled out by someone very familiar with the form. If it is not filled out correctly and if the requirements are not met, then this will add months to the process of your church obtaining 501c3 status. Even when a church hires a certified public accountant or an attorney who specializes in obtaining determination letters, the process (if it goes very smoothly) will normally take several months. If the requirements are not all properly met or if the paperwork is filled out incorrectly, then the process that would normally take 3-6 months, maybe drawn out to more than a year. This process can be led by an attorney or CPA for somewhere in the area of $300-700. A variety of CPA and law firms specialize in this process. The CPA/attorney will inform you of where you need to make changes BEFORE the form is turned in. This will save months. The CPA/attorney will help ensure that your board of directors meets government requirements and that all your verbiage and language are correct in the initial filing. A list of firms that can help with this are included in the appendix section of this book.

Church Bank Accounts, Credit Union Accounts and Management Software

One of the first things you will want to do upon collecting funds, is to correctly and conscientiously handle those funds. You may want to ask your bank or credit union in advance of even your first interest meetings concerning starting a future church, what will be required to open an account. You will probably have the account opened far before you officially receive tax-deductible status, but this is needed because you do want to have a way to properly handle the funds. Getting the bank account opened very early in the church planting process will be to your advantage.

Many small and start-up churches do not see the need in spending money on church accounting software. This is normally a mistake as even a handful of people who are givers will soon compile a long listing of contributions. When the end of the year comes, each giver will need to receive a contribution report. If this has been done by hand on paper or a Word or Pages document, it may suffice temporarily, but you will have done everyone a favor by having the contributions and membership information in a proper database from the day you first received any funds. In today's world, many if not most church management programs are online subscriptions. While this does mean that you will have to pay for this monthly or yearly, it also means that your start-up cost may be as low as $20-40 per month. A few years ago, you had to purchase the entire program, and for a small group this meant that the initial outlay could easily be $450-700 or more. You will appreciate it later if you go ahead and subscribe monthly to a membership and accounting program immediately. If not, at the end of the year, you will probably be surprised at how much time it takes producing those contribution reports. If you have the software in place and someone is keeping up with it every week, then they will simply press a button and produce printed or online contribution reports. It should also be noted that in seven factors that one organization researched, which increase the likelihood of new church success, one of those factors was "systematic efforts to track visitors and prospects." While it may be possible to track visitors and prospects without a capable computer program or app, it is not practical to do so in the world we live in. Several church membership and accounting solutions are listed in the appendix sections of this book, and many of these programs, if not all of them, have the capability to both track attendance, finances, membership, and other vital statistics that assist in building and maintaining a healthy and vibrant congregation.

Denominations, Associations and Church Movements

If your church is affiliated with a denomination, not only will the denomination be interested in helping with these documents, but they often will be able to provide assistance with this initial setup.

Your bishop/superintendent/associational leader will be glad to assist with these documents. They will possibly have sample templates where you simply fill in the blanks and will be a good resource to assist in these areas. Each church must make sure they meet their own associations or denomination's guideline as they set up the local church.

A Note about Assigning People to Leadership Positions too Early

During these initial set up tasks, people may present themselves as good candidates for leadership positions. The people who are helping write the bylaws, constitution and articles of incorporation may likely attempt to put themselves in positions of authority through this process. For this reason, it is highly recommended that these documents are first crafted outside of the local church or launch team meetings. This is another reason why it is a great idea to utilize existing denominational structures, so that power is not invested in people from within the new or still non-existent church. It is almost impossible to discern within a few weeks or months if someone is ready and trustworthy of serious leadership responsibilities. To choose an usher or greeter is one thing, but to determine who will be handling church funds or making decisions with church money is an entirely different issue.

For this reason, the Association of Related Churches (ARC) has set up guidelines for creating healthy church foundational documents. In the ARC approach (which has been extremely successful), most of the power in the church with the exception of the senior pastor is initially coming from OUTSIDE the church. This way, a group of new people cannot highjack the churches' vision from day one. Simultaneously, ARC still has protections for the local church as there are overseers. These pastors, from a distance, not in the local church, have the ability to call the planting pastor's actions into question and if needed, remove the pastor. Similarly, many denominations will set up the local church initially where denominational leaders will have much of the control (along with the local pastor). These scenarios normally are much better for the life of the local church.

The harsh reality is that people who are interested in starting a new church come from all walks of life. Some of them will be coming from other churches where they were disgruntled. If these people were disgruntled at the last church, not always, but sometimes, they had no good reason to be so. Sometimes this person simply cannot get along with people or is generally a trouble maker for pastors. In these cases, they will often try with all their might to grab leadership positions in the formation of a new church. The more of that people grab for power, probably the less likely they should be in power. The more reluctant someone is to take a position of power and responsibility, often these people will be your best church leaders.

3.2 Mission Statements, Vision Statements and Core Values

Churches that do not know where they are going or why they exist will have a difficult time gaining traction with their prospective audience that they desire to convert into a true congregation. Planters that develop strategies for growth, communicate effectively with the use of mission and vision statements and determine the church's core values will fair better with new people looking to identify with a church. In most places in this country, people are not just looking for "a church," they are looking for "their church." There are often many "good" churches in a given community. These "good" churches will not be perfect, but they will, generally speaking, exalt Jesus, teach the Bible, pursue evangelism and discipleship, support various missions projects, and have a reasonable program for children and youth. There will be many commonalities among these churches. In many ways, these "good" churches will be extremely similar. On paper, they may be almost indistinguishable to someone who is not very familiar with Christianity and American church circles. At closer inspection, these churches will have glaring differences.

While these "good" churches may have great fellowship, teaching, music and kids churches, what about their stance on women in ministry, music style, dress code, thoughts on theatrical robotic concert lighting versus traditional chandeliers? Is the church blatantly denominational? Where does the church stand in the light of Wesleyan versus Calvinistic theological debates? The list goes on and on. From style to doctrine, to culture of how everything is done, each church is very unique. When people attend a new church, we will speak loudly to them about who we are from the very moment they step foot on the property. Whether or not they are greeted by friendly people who genuinely meet them in the parking lot, to how clean the restrooms are, and if they feel shunned by those who are already there, who will all make a statement to the guest. If this person has ever attended another church, they will have pre-conceived ideas about how the church should be. It will be close to impossible to fulfill all their expectations, so the friendlier and more welcoming to them that we can be will help them fill in the holes where they may not feel comfortable.

If the guest chooses to return, by week two, at the latest, questions about the new church will begin to arise in their minds. All those questions about who this church is, what it believes, whether or not they fit in there, and how the church operates, in general, will all be at top of mind. When you realize that even the largest churches in the country do not retain all their guests, then you can become more free to be yourself and who God has designed the new church to be. As a guest searches for the answer to all their questions about the church, mission statements, vision statements and core values can help the guest determine if this is the place for them.

Mission Statements

A mission statement defines who the church is and why it exists. The mission statement is different from the vision statement in that the mission statement defines who the church is now and what lies at the core of the church. A vision statement speaks more of what the church can and should become. The mission statement will basically stay the same regardless of the size, age, and success or failure of the church. The vision statement will possibly change and morph as the church develops organizationally. A mission statement might be just a restating or some variation of the Great Commission. Many churches of all sizes choose the Great Commission as their mission statement. Mission statements help us clearly define why we exist and what we should be doing daily. The mission statement of a church using the Great Commission…

First Church exists to go and make disciples of all nations, baptizing them, and teaching them to obey everything Jesus commanded.

An Expanded Mission Statement may look something like: First Church exists to build an assembly of Christian believers who will come to know Jesus Christ personally, grow in His likeness, character and compassion by the transforming presence and person of the Holy Spirit while simultaneously continuing to reach more people who do not know God by engaging them in evangelism and church planting.

The point and purpose in a mission statement like this is to make it clear that the church will not get sidetracked in lots of good activities that are not central to the Gospel. Many churches today have gotten so involved in social issues, political issues and other good things that they have moved the Gospel from the center of the mission of the church. While it is wonderful to clean up neighborhoods or assist with blood drives, these activities are supplementary, not central to the Gospel of Jesus Christ.

The website, Church Relevance has some great thoughts on Church Mission Statements:

"General Findings

- The best mission statements are clear, memorable, and concise.
- Church mission statements are often much too long to remember.
- The average length of the church mission statements here is a full 18.5 words compared to only 15.3 on Top Nonprofit's 50 Example Mission Statements
- The shortest contains only 2 words (Calvary Chapel Ft. Lauderdale)
- The longest mission statement from the this list contains 66 words (Hopewell Missionary Baptist)
- A number of churches base their mission (and/or vision) statements around the great commission, but see the difference between Calvary Chapel Ft. Lauderdale (2 words) and Second Baptist Church's 42 word versions."[12]

Examples of Vision Statements:
Example of a long mission statement from People's Church, Lansing, MI

> *Peoples Church is called to proclaim the Gospel of Christ and the beliefs of the evangelical Christian faith, to maintain the worship of God, and to inspire in all persons a love for Christ, a passion for righteousness, and a consciousness of their duties to God and their fellow human beings. We pledge our lives to Christ and*

---

[12] "50 Examples of Church Mission Statements", https://churchrelevance.com/church-mission-statements-examples/, as accessed May 16, 2019.

covenant with each other to demonstrate His Spirit through worship, witnessing, and ministry to the needs of the people of this church and the community[13]

Below are a list of church mission statement examples and the word count directly after, taken directly from Church Relevance's website. Many of the largest and most famous churches in the country are included…

<u>Calvary Chapel (Ft. Lauderdale, FL)</u>: Making Disciples (2)

<u>Christ Fellowship (Miami, FL)</u>: To make disciples of all nations (6)

<u>Fellowship Church (Grapevine, TX)</u>: To Reach Up, Reach Out, and Reach In (8)

<u>Elevation Church (Matthews, NC)</u>: To see those far from God raised to life in Christ (11)

<u>Celebration Church (Jacksonville, FL)</u>: Leading people to experience a God-First Life (7)

<u>Southeast Christian Church (Louisville, KY)</u>: Connecting people to Jesus and one another (7)

<u>Church of the Highlands (Birmingham, AL)</u>: Reaching people with the life-giving message of Jesus (8)

<u>Seacoast Church (Mt Pleasant, SC)</u>: We exist to help people become fully devoted followers of Christ (11)

---

[13] https://www.missionstatements.com/church_mission_statements.html, as accessed May 16, 2019

Mosaic Church (Hollywood, CA): To Live by Faith, To be Known by Love, and to be a Voice of Hope! (16)

LifeChurch.tv (Edmond, OK): To lead people to become fully devoted followers of Christ (10)

Coral Ridge Presbyterian Church (Ft Lauderdale, FL): We exist to declare and demonstrate the liberating power of the Gospel (12)

The Potter's House (Dallas, TX): We are the voice and the hand that encourages people to change their lives with hope, comfort and peace (19)

Brooklyn Tabernacle (Brooklyn, NY): To spread the Gospel in our community by reaching out in love and respect to people from every nation (19)

Potential Church (Cooper City, FL): Partnering with people to reach their God potential, as they connect with God, become like Christ and influence their world (20)

The Rock (San Diego, CA): Save, Equip, and Send out a highly motivated ARMY of believers who engage every segment of society while remaining true to our DNA (23)

Christ Church of the Valley (Peoria, AZ): To WIN people to Jesus Christ, TRAIN believers to become disciples, and SEND disciples out to impact the world (19)

The Church of the Resurrection UMC (Leawood, KS): To build a Christian community where non-religious and nominally religious people are becoming deeply committed Christians (16)

National Community Church (Washington, DC): To address poverty by assisting the poor, address disease by caring for the sick and address brokenness by transforming through reconciliation (21)

Hillsong (Sydney, Australia): To reach and influence the world by building a large Christ-centred, Bible-based church, changing mindsets and empowering people to lead and impact in every sphere of life (27)

Gateway Church (Southlake, TX): To bring people to Jesus and membership in his family, develop them to Christlike maturity, and equip them for their ministry in the church and life mission in the world, in order to magnify God's name." (36)

Redeemer Presbyterian Church (New York, NY): To build a great city for all people through a gospel movement that brings personal conversion, community formation, social justice and cultural renewal to New York City and, through it, to the world (33)

James River Assembly (Ozark, MO): Our mission is to help lead people into a growing relationship with Jesus Christ by creating a dynamic environment for authentic worship and effective communication while developing genuine community with each other (32)

New Hope Christian Fellowship (Honolulu, HI): To present the Gospel of Jesus Christ in such a way that turns non-Christians into converts, converts into disciples, and disciples into mature, fruitful leaders, who will in turn go into the world and reach others for Christ (38)

Second Baptist Church (Houston, TX): "Go therefore and make disciples of all the nations, baptizing them in the name of the Father and the Son and the Holy spirit, teaching them to observe all that I commanded you; and lo, I am with you always." Matthew 28:19-20 (42)

North Point Community Church (Alpharetta, GA): To lead people into a growing relationship with Jesus Christ." We accomplish our mission by creating environments where people are encouraged and equipped to pursue intimacy with God, community with insiders, and influence with outsiders (35)

Phoenix First Assembly (Phoenix, AZ): To be the church that displays the love of Christ and connects with people of all walks of life through our creative services, discipleship, outreach, and the establishment of multiple campuses by streaming our Weekend Experience services globally (38)

Hopewell Missionary Baptist (Norcross, GA): Fulfill the Great Commission (Matthew 28:19-20) in helping people become fully functioning followers of Christ. Teach the tenets of Christianity. Equip believers for a significant ministry by helping them discover the gifts and talents God gave them (Ephesians 4:11-16). Obey the task that has been given to us by God as a beacon of salvation living out transformational grace through His Son Jesus Christ (Matthew 5:16)" (66)"[14]

Vision Statements

A vision statement can be a blueprint for the churches' preferred future. The vision statement explains what "success" will look like for the local church. The vision statement is sort of like a GPS roadmap. The mission is what you are doing now, and will continue to do every day as a church. The vision is the next major destination of where the church is headed. A GPS tells us where we are going even though we are not there yet. If you press the menu of the GPS it will also show us a "detail view." The Vision Statements' major components are the

---

[14] "50 Examples of Church Mission Statements", https://churchrelevance.com/church-mission-statements-examples/, as accessed May 16, 2019.

"detail view" turn by turn directions of what the process of moving toward becoming the church that God wants us to be will look like.

Thom Ranier, former president and CEO of Lifeway resources recommends the following when crafting a church vision statement: *The six elements of a church vision statement are: 1. The vision statement must be biblical 2. Have the vision statement mirror your discipleship process 3. Keep the vision statement succinct and memorable 4. Ensure your ministries align with the vision statement 5. Develop an ongoing vehicle to communicate the vision statement to the members (front end, continuous) 6. Communicate expectations of the members in the vision statement*[15]

Below are examples of church vision statements, again, these are directly from Church Relevance website. They did such an excellent job, compiling great examples, I saw no reason to redo a list.

Christ Fellowship (Miami, FL): *To make disciples of all nations. (6 words)*

Christ Church of the Valley (Peoria, AZ): *Impacting 100,000 Phoenix area residents by the year 2020. (9)*

The Rock (San Diego, CA): *To be a global and highly trusted model of relevant and innovative evangelism. (13)*

The Potter's House (Dallas, TX): *We are the voice and the hand that encourages people to change their lives with hope, comfort and peace. (19)*

---

[15] Thom S. Rainer's Blog, *Growing Healthy Churches. Together.* As accessed May 16, 2019. "Crafting a Church Vision Statement", https://thomrainer.com/2015/07/crafting-a-church-vision-statement-rainer-on-leadership-143/

NewSpring Church (Anderson, SC): To continue growing, impacting lives and using technology and the arts to reach 100,000 people for Jesus Christ. (18)

Willow Creek (South Barrington, IL): We believe all people matter to God and that Christ's message and ministry through the local church is the hope of the world. (23)

Coral Ridge Prespyterian Church (Ft Lauderdale, FL): To rescue and replenish a world lost and broken by sin, thereby "making all things new" (Revelation 21:5). (19)

Kensington Community Church (Troy, MI): To turn people who think God is irrelevant into fully devoted followers of Jesus Christ through high-impact churches. (19)

Gateway Church (Southlake, TX): To bring people to Jesus and membership in his family, develop them to Christlike maturity, and equip them for their ministry in the church and life mission in the world, in order to magnify God's name."(36)

Redeemer Presbyterian Church (New York, NY): To build a great city for all people through a gospel movement that brings personal conversion, community formation, social justice and cultural renewal to New York City and, through it, to the world. (33)

Phoenix First (Phoenix, AZ): To be the church that displays the love of Christ and connects with people of all walks of life through our creative services, discipleship, outreach, and the establishment of multiple campuses by streaming our Weekend Experience services globally. (38)

Celebration Church (Jacksonville, FL): "Therefore go make disciples of all nations, baptizing them in the name of the Father, and of the Son, *and of the Holy Spirit, and teaching them to obey everything I have commanded you. And surely I am with you, always, to the end of the age." -Matthew 28:19-20 NIV (50)*

<u>Saddleback (Lake Forest, CA)</u>: *"It is the dream of a place where the hurting, the depressed, the frustrated, and the confused can find love, acceptance, help, hope, forgiveness, guidance, and encouragement.*

It is the dream of sharing the Good News of Jesus Christ with the hundreds of thousands of residents in south Orange County.

It is the dream of welcoming 20,000 members into the fellowship of our church family-loving, learning, laughing, and living in harmony together.

It is the dream of developing people to spiritual maturity through Bible studies, small groups, seminars, retreats, and a Bible school for our members.

It is the dream of equipping every believer for a significant ministry by helping them discover the gifts and talents God gave them.

It is the dream of sending out hundreds of career missionaries and church workers all around the world, and empowering every member for a personal life mission in the world. It is the dream of sending our members by the thousands on short-term mission projects to every continent. It is the dream of starting at least one new daughter church every year.

It is the dream of at least fifty acres of land, on which will be built a regional church for south Orange County-with beautiful, yet simple, facilities including a worship center seating thousands, a counseling and prayer center, classrooms for Bible studies and training lay ministers, and a recreation area. All of this will be designed to minister to the local person -spiritually, emotionally physically, and socially-and set in a peaceful, inspiring garden landscape." (254)

<u>Hillsong (Sydney, Australia)</u>: "The Church that I see is a Church of influence. A Church so large in size that the city and nation cannot ignore it. A Church growing so quickly that buildings struggle to contain the increase.

I see a Church whose heartfelt praise and worship touches Heaven and changes earth; worship which influences the praises of people throughout the earth, exalting Christ with powerful songs of faith and hope.

I see a Church whose altars are constantly filled with repentant sinners responding to Christ's call to salvation.

Yes, the Church that I see is so dependent on the Holy Spirit that nothing will stop it nor stand against it; a Church whose people are unified, praying and full of God's Spirit.

The Church that I see has a message so clear that lives are changed forever and potential is fulfilled through the power of His Word; a message beamed to the peoples of the earth through their television screens.

I see a Church so compassionate that people are drawn from impossible situations into a loving and friendly circle of hope, where answers are found and acceptance is given.

I see a people so Kingdom-minded that they will count whatever the cost and pay whatever the price to see revival sweep this land.

The Church that I see is a Church so committed to raising, training and empowering a leadership generation to reap the end-time harvest that all its ministries are consumed with this goal.

I see a Church whose head is Jesus, whose help is the Holy Spirit and whose focus is the Great Commission.

YES, THE CHURCH THAT I SEE COULD WELL BE OUR CHURCH – HILLSONG CHURCH." (279)[16]

Observations about Mission and Vision Statements: of the churches which appear on both of the above lists, some churches get far wordier when it comes to vision statements than mission statements. Most noticeably, Hillsongs Church has a 27-word mission statement and a 279-word vision statement (over ten times the length of the mission statement). Regardless of how one feels about Hillsong's style or theology, they have organizationally multiplied to the point where recently they have formed their own new denomination. So, while general wisdom is to keep a mission and vision statement short and succinct - length, at least when it comes to a vision statement, sometimes works as well. The mission statements of churches should be more universally similar, as ultimately, every church is called to fulfill the Great Commission. The vision statement of each individual church will be more diverse. Often vision statements reflect the pastors, people, style, culture, and location of each church. The vision statement will greatly influence the final product of what a given church will look and feel like. Each pastor is responsible for hearing from God on the vision and crafting that vision in time with the help and under the guidance of the Holy Spirit.

---

[16] Craig Van Korlaar, "30+ Examples of Church Vision Statements", ChurchRelevance.com, https://churchrelevance.com/30-church-vision-statements-examples/, as accessed May 16, 2019.

Core Values

Core values are an important component for defining how a church operates and what the church truly takes seriously. Sometimes core values are also expressed as simply "values" or "codes." Many churches say one set of things are their core values but actually show by their actions that what they say and what they believe are two different things altogether.

A pastor who comes into a church or starts a church by clearly stating the church's core values (as many churches already somewhat do with vision and mission statements), has a greater chance of leading the church to success than a leader who haphazardly goes about this process or does not think it through and leaves it totally up to chance.

One church that stands out in the discussion of core values is Crossroads World Outreach Center in West Columbia, SC under the leadership of Pastor Tim Hodge. In traveling to more than 100 churches of all sizes in the last couple of years, this is the only church that I have seen to have their core values clearly, publicly stated. They have a large flag banner, prominently displayed in their lobby listing these values. The Crossroads Church lists the following as core values: Excellence, Significance, Passion, Consistency, Accountability, Humility, Character and Radical. Core values take it a step further and actually spells out for people a little bit about the flavor of the church. For example, when a church says "Excellence," you immediately know that while they are not perfect, they are at least aiming to glorify God with their services' organization, facility's cleanliness, and offering a variety of activities and ecclesiastical programs. "Significance" lets you know they are not just looking for "success," but the right kind of success. "Consistency" caught my attention, as I was thinking this is one that I can struggle with from time to time.

Core values help to define us and gives the vision and mission steering principles and means by which to propel the church forward. While vision and mission are the organizational engine which drives the church, the core values are similar to a transmission that assists in transmitting the power from the engine to the people of the fellowship in order to move the church forward.

A couple of examples of the core values of large, prominent churches - Prestonwood and Elevation. Prestonwood Baptist Church, Plano, Texas lists its core values as: excellence, evangelism, engagement, equipping, expansion and encouragement. An explanation of each value is listed in paragraph form on their website.[17] Elevation Church, Matthews, North Carolina, lists their values as their "Code." The code includes ten points:

> *1. Jesus is the center. It's about: Integrated Priorities 2. We believe big and start small. It's about: Active Faith 3. We honor one another to glorify God. It's about: Valuing People 4. We are contributors, not consumers. It's about: Taking Action 5. We think inside the box. It's about: Embracing Limitation 6. We can do more by doing less. It's about: Focused Excellence 7. We don't maintain, we multiply. It's about: Ongoing Growth 8. We eat the fish and leave the bones. It's about: Teachable Attitudes 9. We want to be known for what we are for. It's about: Promoting Unity 10. We will not take this for granted. It's about: Expressing Gratitude.*[18] Elevation lists their mission and vision

---

[17] "Our Core Values", Prestonwood Baptist Church, Plano, Texas, http://www.prestonwood.org/about/our-core-values, as accessed May 16, 2019.

[18] "Keeping the Vision Clear", Elevation Church, Matthews, North Carolina, https://elevationchurch.org/values/, as accessed May 16, 2019.

statements on the same page, which are extremely simple. *Mission Statement: Elevation Church exists so that people far from God will be raised to life in Christ.*

Vision Statement: See what God can do through you.[19]

They say much more with their "code" than they actually do with their mission and vision statements.

Crafting a compelling mission and vision statement should be a part of each church planters pre-launch process. The trend in large, growing churches seems to be brief mission statements with slightly longer vision statements. While many churches do not list core values, they may also be helpful to your church to think through. Mission and vision statements are not the secret weapon to church growth, but they can be a framework to think through what it is God has called your specific church to be. Sometimes churches gain a high level of success with no official mission, vision or core values statements. This is mentioned because some churches spend large amounts of time crafting a list of statements that are then not put into practice. The statements are a framework for doing the work of the Kingdom, but the statements do not do the work for you. May the Lord help you design statements that will be of assistance to those who are wondering what makes your church tick, and then may the Lord help us get to work, doing the wonderful work of the ministry.

3.3 Forming a Launch Team

Forming a launch team is a critical element in the life of the future church. The launch team will help you recruit and invite other potential church launch team members and future church members, they will do much of the groundwork when it comes to setting up

---

[19] Elevation Church, https://elevationchurch.org/values/

and tearing down in a portable situation of a school, or theater, this team will serve as prayer warriors to spiritually cover the new work, they will man children's ministries, ushering, greeting, music ministry, sound/lighting/video tech team and much more. Without a good launch team, the future prospects of the church are greatly diminished. The Association of Related Churches (ARC) who have launched more than 800 churches in the last two decades with great success, in most cases, requires the planter to have secured a launch team of 35 people before they will release funds to plant a church. ARC believes that for a church to be successful, it will take an average of about 35 people to make a minimum launch team if you are planning to "launch large." These 35 people will be organized into the basic group of greeters, ushers, children's ministry team, music team, tech team, and everything else that needs to be accomplished in the life of a new church.

Critical mass

A component in the discussion of the launch team discussion is critical mass. Critical mass has to do with the "feel" of the new church. The size of the crowd communicates to the potential church members something about what the general Sunday expectation of the future will be, how available the pastor will be, how successful and influential the future will be and if the church will have enough people to impact their community in a meaningful way. When churches are started with less than 35 people, the chances of them remaining relatively small for a long period of time is great. If a church has a launch team of 35 people, it is very possible that between inviting people by word of mouth, social media marketing, mass mail marketing, and other forms of communication that the first service may have 200-400 people in attendance. When about 200 people fill a room, trouble makers have less influence. Normally, the larger the crowd, the less likely extreme trouble makers will get into leadership at the church. If a church only has 15-25 people, anyone would assume they could easily and quickly get into leadership. If a church has 30 people, many people will assume that the members will have 100% unfettered access to the pastor 24 hours a day, 7 days a week. While it is good for a pastor to care for his people, small churches that depend on their pastor for everything tend to remain very small because no one else gets involved in doing the actual work of the ministry. On the other hand, if people are taught and realize upfront that the pastor does not and will not do everything, then either they will leave (because they have small church expectations and cannot get their way) or they will stay and be more likely to get involved. Forward-thinking people quickly realize that if they do not participate in the work of the ministry, then the church will never reach its potential. People that desire the pastor to do all the ministry have both an unhealthy and unbiblical view of the church which will be covered later in "Church Member Leadership Roles."

Critical mass also plays an important role in the long term viability of the church. Studies have shown time and again that approximately 100 people are needed to sustain a congregation long term. While there are many hundreds of thousands of churches that have 30-50 members and do fine, many of these churches did not start that way. Many small churches today occupy a building that in its initial years, had around 100 people attending. One hundred people often, pay the pastor a full-time salary, build a church building or two, and build a parsonage. Over time, even if the church dwindles down to 20 people or so, the buildings and parsonages are paid off. This allows even a very small church to sustain itself and pay a pastor either a meager full-time salary or a healthy part-time salary.

If in the initial years (say year one to five), the church, on the other hand, does not at least approach the 100 people mark, many times the high cost of rent or mortgage will shut the church down. If the church does not reach 100 people in the first five years, often it will die in those first five years or shortly thereafter. This is another reason that critical mass is important. ARC believes so strongly in this because if the church can reach 200-300 people or better on launch day, even with average new church attrition (losing 50-60% of launch day numbers in the following month after the launch), the group will still have around 100 almost from the very start.

Critical mass for the launch team may not need to be as high of a number as 35 people if you are in a demographically small situation. If your town has 500 people and the town is not a suburb of a mid-sized city, then it may not be realistic to require a launch team of 35. Even in a town of 500, a launch team of 35 or more would be preferable, but if you have 15 after six months of trying to assemble a launch team, then this may be what you have to go with. In a situation like this, expectations will need to be adjusted, and the pastor will probably need to plan to be bi-vocationally (at least holding down a part-time job) for the foreseeable future. Whatever the situation, as captain obvious would say, "The more people, the better!"

How to Assemble a Launch Team

The most common thought currently on assembling a launch team from scratch is probably "interest socials." An interest social is a gathering where free food is provided, and then at the end of about a one-hour gathering, the potential pastor gives a very brief talk about his dream church. The Association of Related Churches teaches interest meetings and socials as the preferred way to gather the initial launch team. The attendees of the social are then given a card where they can mark that either a) they are not interested b) they would like more information about the potential church and would like to eat lunch or breakfast with the planter to discuss things or c) they are completely on board already and just need direction as to how to sign up. The socials may be an ice cream tasting party with 25 flavors of free ice cream, a Bar-B-Q lunch, or something else that the local demographic might be interested in. Sometimes, a planter will move into an apartment complex with a commons area that can be rented to hold such a party.

Other planters with young children have found success by recruiting from other parents in their age group through children's sporting events. A kids' community soccer team, for example, may be a good place to find young families looking to get themselves and their children involved in church. It is worth noting that this is NOT recommended for people who do not have kids involved in sports as this would surely come off as very strange to say the least.

Some churches have found success by having a large group of people move in mass to a city to plant a church. While this may work very well as you will already have a committed core, there is possibly a negative to this setup. If a high-level leader (perhaps the long term associate or youth pastor of a megachurch) can convince 20-30 people to change jobs and uproot their family to move to another city to start a church with them, this seems powerful on the surface for church planting. When this does occur, many times, it produces an incredible new church in the city.

If you consider who would be moving several states away with a popular pastor or youth pastor, you may be able to spot the problem. All these people were going to the same church and youth ministry together already, many of them for years. The relationship with this pastor and the people who are following them is very strong. Most of these people are super committed to the Lord and the Church. When they move into the new city, there is little need to make new relationships because they brought several mature, strong relationships with them to the city already. In this case, sometimes these very committed people will show up at pre-launch meetings, interest meetings, and church services to be certain. Since these relationships are already formed, they may not see the same need to build new ones. If the committed people do not reach out very purposefully to the new community, they will be of little help to the planter and the plant. If someone moves into a city with no friends or relationships, it is imperative, almost for their own social survival, that they make new friends. In these instances, the chances of church planting success may be greater. If one does move with a pre-established group, it will be very important that the pastor continually calls the members to reach out and evangelize like their life depended on it, because the life of their future church will depend on it!

Other Launch Team Thoughts

The terminology of launch team is preferred for several reasons over the wording of "Core Group." Core group has fallen out of favor in church planting circles in part because it implies that the group is important and essential to the life of the future church. While all people are important, and the launch team is very important, all people are not important to the long-term future of the church. In fact, some people will need to move on for the health of the church. If people are told they are the core team, to some, this will fill a possibly, unhealthy need for importance. Unfortunately, some people will hoard positions, guard against new people who are talented that may threaten them, and generally keep others from easily finding their place in the new church. Another reason that the term "launch team" is preferred has to do with the normal rate at which people leave new churches. As hard as it is to say, many people that are with a new church and planter at year one will not be with the church in year two and year three. There is nothing wrong with the fact that people will move on. It is sad for the church planter (most of the time), but many people will see how the culture of the church is forming and will realize that they do not fit in or they do not prefer the church long-term. Others may move because of job transfers out of state. People leave for a myriad of reasons, but people will leave the new plant. For growth, the key is just to keep more coming in the front door than are going out the back door. The term launch group also can assist in insuring that people are not permanently put into positions until we know them well. We may be tempted as a church planter to promise someone a position or give someone a title in order to keep them around, but when someone is placed in a position in the initial formation days, they may not be the best person for that position in just a matter of months.

3.4 Church Member Leadership Roles

The New Testament model of church planting and organization makes it very clear that the fivefold ministry leaders are called to equip others (the church membership) to do the work of the ministry.

> *And He gave some as apostles, and some as prophets, and some as evangelists, and some as pastors and teachers, for the equipping of the saints for the work of service, to the building up of the body of Christ; until we all attain to the unity of the faith, and of the knowledge of the Son of God, to a mature man, to the measure of the stature which belongs to the fullness of Christ.*
> **Ephesians 4:11-13 New American Standard Bible**

Also, deacons are called, not to make business decisions, but to do the actual work of the ministry, such as the daily distribution of bread.

> *Then the twelve summoned the multitude of the disciples and said, "It is not desirable that we should leave the word of God and **serve** tables. Therefore, brethren, seek out from among you seven men of good reputation, full of the Holy Spirit and wisdom, whom we may appoint over this business; but we will give ourselves continually to prayer and to the ministry of the word." And the saying pleased the whole multitude. And they chose Stephen, a man full of faith and the Holy Spirit, and Philip, Prochorus, Nicanor, Timon, Parmenas, and Nicolas, a proselyte from Antioch, whom they set before the apostles; and when they had prayed, they laid hands on them.* **Acts 6:2-6 New King James Version**

The term "serve" here in these verses is where we get the term deacon. From the Greek, the term is diakoneō which literally means to serve. In this instance, it is in the sense of serving tables as a waiter or waitress. Amazingly, many people consider the role of deacons to be advising and sometimes even controlling the pastor. Never in the scripture is this the case. If a deacon is to serve in a board or council capacity, this should always be a secondary function. The role is primarily to help people in the church through service, care, concern, and prayer. Deacons should be about the business of keeping up with members, visiting the hospitals and homes of the sick, checking on widows, cutting the grass at church and such activities. Deacons are not to primarily lead the church in matters of finances; if a deacon is a decision-maker, this should be a secondary part of their calling.

When the church is being formed, it will be easiest to properly define the roles of pastor, deacons, elders, youth director, etc. If these are thoughtfully and carefully defined, then there is hopefully less of a likelihood for confusion in these roles in the long term life of the church. The more important the role, the more authority it will come with, the longer the church should wait to install people into these positions. At Harvest Christian Center, we waited more than five years before installing any elders or deacons. This allowed us to know the people relatively well. Even then, you are praying and doing the best you can. Sometimes people can be deceitful and put on a "good show," so the longer the church has to know those who labor among them, the better.

As the church develops each volunteer and eventually each paid position in the church hierarchy, it is wisdom to develop a written job description for each position. The more complicated the position, the more detailed the job description should be. The process to become an elder in a church (or an equivalent leading position that may have a different title) should be especially well thought out. A process of nomination, with the inner circle of leadership, then having the ability to remove any unqualified candidates from the mix before the church later votes on them is a good thing. For example, one time a seemingly very "nice guy" in the church was nominated as a deacon. We had a rule that once a deacon or elder was nominated that there was a period between nomination and the time that the church would approve the people by church vote. One of the men that were nominated, I knew from counseling, while he had repented, within the last year, he had abused his wife physically. While he may have appeared to be a "nice guy" with a big smile, he certainly was not qualified to lead the church in any spiritual capacity. Thankfully, over the next three years or so, we saw this man truly dedicated his life to Christ. He apologized to his wife for his deplorable behavior and went on to become a MUCH better husband. Even though he changed greatly, he certainly was in no way ready to take on a leadership in the church when he was first nominated to do so. If the church had not had a system in place to stop possible bad congregational nominations, then this man would have been a deacon in a relatively short period of time. While we certainly made some mistakes with choosing leadership, on this occasion, we were thankfully able to root this person out of the process before the church was able to vote on them.

3.5 Church Marketing

Church marketing is considered a dirty word by some pastors who believe that somehow it is unspiritual. The definition of marketing is relatively simple - promoting or selling products or services. Now while some may shy away from considering the Church or Jesus as a "product," the question is, is He worth promoting? We do not sell Jesus, we give Him away, but surely He is worth promoting more than Coca-cola, the latest movie, your favorite brand of athletic shoes or any other product on the planet. Church marketing is simply a means of getting the word out to more people, and when starting a church, adding an additional church service, revitalizing an old dying church, or expanding by adding a new church campus location, marketing is essential in the 2020s and beyond.

Common Types of Church Marketing:

Website - years ago, the church building's property was the guests first impression. While the property should have well-manicured grounds and a building that is neat and clean in appearance, the church website is now the first marketing impression for many, if not most of your potential members. If the website appears dated in appearance or if it contains calendar information that is actually out of date, this will send the wrong impression to potential attendees. Money spent on building a great website is a very good investment. If the church has no money for any other marketing, at a minimum, the church should have a great website. Today, many companies offer templates and will even have people build the site for your church for surprisingly low rates. Occasionally, older pastors who lead churches of less than 20 people ask me about growing their churches. There is a desire to grow, but these same pastors do not have websites. They have a difficult time understanding that virtually everyone will first look at your website and social sites before they decide to attend your church. If the church has no online presence, then the chances that anyone will visit are very low. When starting a church in the 2020s, the initial website investment is of utmost importance. Paying people to design it well, making it fast and responsive, having your keywords for search engine optimized are all important parts of the process. While it may not be needed to spend multiple thousands and thousands of dollars on your site, it will probably be needful to at least spend several hundred. Whatever you do and however much you spend, make sure that the website is the best you can possibly make it for the budget that you have. The marketing budget should be reflected in the website and social media marketing probably before the money is spent on any other type of marketing in the 2020s.

Social media - facebook, instagram, youtube and new social media sites that will become popular over the years to come are essential to promote a church. Most all of these services have options where a church can pay to target specific demographics in their area and market directly to them. Unlike mass marketing of the past (television, radio), social media marketing can be done in a much more cost-effective manner. Utilizing age groups, location and what people like and dislike, marketing can be zeroed in on exactly who is most likely to respond to an advertisement from your church. In the past, mass marketing was very expensive as you had no control over who would see your ad. Today, the potential audience is controlled, and the cost is much less. You can boost posts for just a few dollars. While church planters will probably want to invest thousands of dollars into social media marketing, it is possible to just spend a small amount which is not possible with mass marketing.

Mass mail - direct mail gets a bad rap as we move more and more toward other forms of electronic media and away from the traditional, physical mailbox, While it is true that mail plays less and less of an importance to many Americans, it is still a viable media form. I am a little bias toward mass mail because the church that I planted and pastored for 14 years was built primarily off of mass mail. From starting with an extremely modest 6,000 piece, black and white mailout that we prepared ourselves in the year 2000 to eventually sending several 50,000 piece mailers as the church developed, we saw countless success stories from mass mail. Even today, the Association of Related Churches (ARC) still encourages mass mail. The numbers are now possible as low as 1/4 of a percent visit rate (10,000 pieces should yield 25 visitors). However, this is on the low side of things, and your percentage may be much higher. Many people read that number and think, why would I ever mess with that? If you convert 10 of those 25 people into giving members, it will be a relatively short period of time before that initial mail investment is returned. Likewise, if you send out 100,000 pieces and get 250 people to attend, you may be able to get 100 people to convert into regular attendees. The financial investment numbers seem large, but if you can get those people to convert to regular attendees and then members, it can be very rewarding. Yes, occasionally a mail out will go bad, and basically no one will attend, but most of the time, this can be avoided. If you are going to put large money into a mailer, be certain to have an experienced group of people that have started churches check and triple check the mailer for accuracy, design quality, communication, and a myriad of other details that need to be examined. For example, as someone who has literally probably sent out over 500,000 pieces of mail, I can tell you of a horror story. One time, we sent out 45,000 pieces without a date advertised on the mailer. So we had this big day planned at church, but never told them what date we wanted people to attend. Because of this, almost no one from that mailer attended at all. This kind of mistake would have been absolutely devastating if we had been starting the church and all of our money would have been invested in that one piece. When we at that point had about 300 people weekly, it was a big, stupid deal, but it was not nearly as devastating as it would have been if we had been in the initial stages of the church plant years before. ARC requires potential church planters to have their mailer approved by their mentors before the funds for the mailer are approved. The message of the mailer is also important. If it is too exclusive, you will rule out a lot of people before they ever attend the church. If you cast a wide net, you may be surprised who will visit and begin attending the church. Outreach Marketing is a great company that still specializes in mass mail. There are many other great mass mail companies as well.

Mass Phone calls - while it is not as common as it once was, some church plants have had great success in the past with calling people to invite them. In the day we live in with so many robocalls, the do not call registry and scams, this will probably not be the best idea unless someone is especially skilled in this area.

Invite cards - custom printed invitation cards that match website, social media and website graphics are a great way to invite launch team members or church members family and friends. Outreach Marketing and many other companies provide matching invite cards. Importantly, invite cards also provide a way to easily get your people individually involved in outreach and evangelism. Occasionally invite cards may lead to a meaningful conversation about Jesus or spiritual needs. Invite cards can serve a dual purpose. When just a few cards are handed out by those doing the inviting, the launch team or church member can concentrate on their close friends and family who are more likely to attend anyway. Naturally outgoing team members can be given large numbers of invite cards and while these may not have as high rate of a response from people they do not know, when an invite card is given to someone who may have already received some other form of marketing (mass mail, social, etc.), this may dramatically increase the chance of this person attending when they have a person face to face invitation.

Television and Radio - these mediums are not what they once were. They still have their place, but today most people are receiving the modern equivalent of television and radio on their phones or personal devices. If you are going to use tv and radio, try to get educated on the way it works in your local market. It is very important to get ratings from the stations you use. Some Christian stations will not provide ratings. This is often because the local secular stations have an audience that can be ten to twenty times larger. Often a 30-second spot on secular radio will reach more than 20 spots on a Christian station. The prices of the advertisement should reflect this, or there is often no good financial reason to utilize the Christian station over the secular one.

Print advertising - newspapers, coupon flyers and the like obviously have an ever diminishing place in modern life. Twenty years ago, anyone starting a church would have rented space in a local paper. Most of this money today, should probably be re-routed to the website and social media. If you are utilizing the newspaper, make sure ample funds have first been allocated to digital advertising.

Billboards - are more of a branding feature than something that directly and solely brings someone to your church. You should only do billboards if your church has first saturated your market with almost all other types of advertisement. If you do choose to use a billboard, do not put more information on it than there should be. Some churches load a billboard with all kinds of crazy information.

You cannot read it going 55 miles per hour. This is silly. A billboard is designed for a very brief amount of information that can be read in an instant - the churches' name, a brief catchphrase or directional arrow to turn on a road are about all that makes sense on a billboard.

Yard signs - are a nice touch for a large campaign. Keep in mind that cities have ordinances that often limit where these signs can be planted. Your church can be fined if these signs are out of code, for example, in many road rights of ways.

3.6 Staffing

When planting a new church, staffing will be a consideration if you are considering the large launch model. **Church secretary/ administrative person** - Most people will recommend having an administration person early on. The keeping of proper records of attendance, following up on guests, financial accounting and other basic administrative tasks will need to be handled with care very early on in the process. Many wise pastors (including Dr. Paul Walker, the former pastor of Atlanta's Mount Paran Church of God) taught that hiring an excellent secretary is the first hire that should be made outside of the pastor. A great administrative person can make all the difference in the world. From the start, this may not need to be a 40 hour per week position, but a 10-20 hour of week position can revolutionize the work output and efficiency of a church office. Today, many company's offer virtual assistants. A virtual assistant is not necessarily a program like Siri on your phone, but a virtual assistant may be a real person that works remotely. These professionals can be hired by the hour and will only need to be hired for the actual man hours that your church is needing. Many churches are today hiring virtual assistants and other contractor type part-time positions out to remote professionals in the fields of graphic design, videography, and the church management fields. There are even companies that do nothing but provide video announcements for churches remotely. However, churches decide to do it, a well-organized church "office" (even if it is a virtual one) will greatly increase the possibility of church growth.

Hiring from within - in his book *Launch,* Nelson Searcy discusses in his staffing section the ideas of hiring from within and the value of the $50 staff member. Many large and mega-churches only hire from within. The concept is that it is easier to control the culture of the church if you only hire from within. Peter Drucker says, "Culture eats strategy for breakfast." Maintaining the churches' desired culture is far more important and at the same time more difficult to do than just hiring a competent worker or pastor. If you hire from within, you will have had the opportunity to see someone in your environment, know how they interact with others and determine if you will be able to have ministry chemistry with them. Many staff pastors have experienced great success in one church setting, and then they will move to another church and be a total flop. This is often a result of the fact that while they are a stellar worker, they simply do not fit the next church where they are employed. If you met two youth pastors who both worked at churches of 500 and had over 200 youth attending their main youth services, you would probably rightly assume that both are gifted and dedicated pastors. Let's say that one of those youth pastors worked at a rural King James only, where the pastor wore a coat and tie to church in a small town in the South. Let's say that the other youth pastor worked at an attractional style church in a city of more than one million where the senior pastor has the sides of his head shaved and preached in skinny jeans from the Message Bible in the Northeast. If you switched those two youth pastors, you would probably have a major disaster in your youth ministry. While those may be extreme culture differences, there are a million minor shades of church culture that permeate each local church fellowship. The more that continuity of ministry style and thought can be maintained, the greater the chances that the church will succeed.

Nelson Searcy also discusses the $50 staff member. Searcy suggests that there are people that you can pay $50 a week to stabilize very important volunteer staff positions. For example, if you are in a mobile church situation, setting up and tearing down weekly in a school - there are certain people that you cannot afford to not be able to know if they will be dependable or not. If the person responsible for bringing the sound system to the school just decides to stay home or not show up on time, this could be a major disaster for the day. Hopefully, a church will have several levels of volunteer contingencies in place where various people will cover if the sound guy and sound equipment did not show up, but if the sound guy is making $50 a week, there is possibly a slightly higher chance that he will show up. Also, if the $50 a week guy knows the $50 can be removed, while for most people this will not be a make or break amount of money, it will maintain some people slightly longer if they consider that the church "job" is basically covering their families phone bill for the month or maybe they are helping make half a car payment.

The other thing that Searcy mentions is that the person in a $50 a week job can be easily watched and courted for other full-time positions in the church. If a volunteer shows a large amount of commitment and promise, they can be moved into a $50 a week position. If a $50 a week person does well in this limited position, they can be moved into a higher staff position later. In my ministry, in the past in Florida, we had several people that received between $200 and $300 a month. This worked very well, just as Searcy says it did in his New York City church.

PART II

CHURCH PLANTING MODELS, CHINESE HOUSE CHURCHES AND DENOMINATIONAL APPROACHES

CHAPTER 4

CHURCH PLANTING MODELS AND MOVEMENT

Church planting is vital for the Church as a whole. When considering the importance of starting new churches, it is useful to consider that, in David Olson's book, *The American Church in Crisis*, "estimates 'that this year in America 3,200 churches will stop functioning...[and] 4,000 churches will be planted.'"[20] Church planting is to the Church as conception and giving birth are to any species on the planet - without reproduction; eventually you die. It is a risky undertaking that requires calling, finances, skill and strategy, yet it is the only way the Church can grow globally. Church planting is good for everyone involved. Studies have shown that attending worship services decreases the mortality rates of the participants.[21] Whether it is purely spiritual, a result of

---

[20] Grigg, Ty, book review, "Starting Missional Churches: life with God in the neighborhood" (Evangelical Missions Quarterly); 51 no 3 Jul 2015, p. 351, ALTA Religion Database. accessed November 18, 2018.

[21] Krause, N, "Invited Commentary: Explaining the Relationship Between Attending Worship Services and Mortality- A Brief Excursion Into the Contribution of Social Relationships in Religious Institutions" (American Journal of Epidemiology; 2017 Apr 01, Vol. 185 Issue 7), p. 524. accessed November 18, 2018. http://doi.org/10.1093/aje/kww180

social relationships or some other unknown factor, attending church services cause people to live longer; even an atheist could receive a benefit of church attendance.

In today's world, there are a number of models and strategies for church planting. These include traditional models, large launch/attractional, missional, house churches, and multi-site models. We will deal extensively with house churches, especially in Asia. We will also look at denominational strategies of church planting, missional churches, and urban/global city church planting.

4.1 Overview of Five Types of Church Planting Models and Movements

Once a church planter gets their calling and foundation worked out, then it's time to determine what church planting model the planter will be working with. Currently, there are at least five models of church planting around the world. These include Traditional, Large Launch/Launch Big or Attractional, Missional Incarnational, Organic, and Multi-site/Satellite Campus[22].

4.2 The Traditional Model

is relatively simple. The idea is that an enthusiastic planter moves into a community, starts sharing the Gospel with everyone he meets, and eventually starts having worship services. Ed Stetzer recommends having at least four families and some type of music before you begin

---

[22] Stetzer, Ed. 2018. "Finding the right Church Plant Model: An Introduction to Church Models (Part 1)." Edstetzer.com, December 26, 2018. Accessed February 22, 2019. https://edstetzer.com/2018/12/finding-the-right-church-plant-model-an-introduction-to-church-models-part-1/?mc_cid=ea0deb17ed&mc_eid=0f-447d78ed

having "worship services."[23] From the worship services, small groups or Sunday school begins to flow. This model often involves pastors who are bi-vocational at first, and the group may possibly grow into a more established church in time. These churches are often adopted by denominations who come alongside the planter and offer financial support and buildings in exchange for their denominational affiliation and loyalty. Stetzer also notes that this model is often used among minority groups because the planter will already have an in-roads into the community (especially in foreign language minority groups in large urban areas).

The church that I started successfully, was basically the traditional model with a touch of the large launch model that is next to be discussed. We started having worship services immediately (even though we only had 11 people). About four months in (now having about 25 people attending), we launched the church with all we could afford which was a 6,000 piece mail-out. The mail-out helped us jump in attendance to about 55 people on the launch week which brought momentum as we simultaneously moved into a small church building (moving out of a very small hotel conference room). After the launch week, we started running about 45 on a low day and grew to about 60 over the next 6 months. Then, we were able to merge with another church, which again caused momentum and pushed the church to around 100 people most of the time. We were able to build a building in the next two years which helped us run 150+ weekly before going to multiple services.

---

[23] Stetzer, Ed. 2019. "Finding the right Church Plant Model: The Traditional Model (Part 2)." Edstetzer.com, January 3, 2019. Accessed February 22, 2019. https://edstetzer.com/2019/01/finding-the-right-church-plant-model-the-traditional-model-part-2/?mc_cid=6d4694e95f&mc_eid=0f447d78ed

Strengths of the Traditional Model:
low financial investment, limited personnel needed

Weaknesses of the Traditional Model:
this model may take a long time to get off the ground

4.3 The Large Launch/Attractional Model

is very popular today among many church planting organizations. Rick Warren's Purpose Driven Church described his massive success several decades ago, and many have copied him to this day. In recent years, this model has proven monumentally successful for the Association of Related Churches (ARC), which was founded by Seacoast Church in South Carolina. ARC was founded by Pastor Greg Surratt of Seacoast Church, who partnered with Chris Hodges (who founded Church of the Highlands, Birmingham, AL) and Rick Bezet (who founded New Life Church, Conway, AR) in the early 2000s. As of early 2019, ARC claims to have planted more than 800 churches with a more than 93% success rate making ARC experts on the large launch model. The large launch involves building a launch team of dedicated adults who are willing/attractional to help you get a church off the ground. The ARC will not fund anyone to plant a church until their launch team has at least 35 committed adults involved.[24] The large launch gathers a team through interest meetings (ice cream socials, BBQs, etc.) over the course of a year and then trains this team to prepare for a large launch day. After moving to the city where they will plant, ideally, every two to four weeks the planter holds a social gathering with food where the goal is to have 20-30 people attend this Interest Event. At the end of the event, the planter speaks for about ten minutes concerning why they want to start a church. The attendees are asked to fill out a card indicating one of three items. Either

---

[24] ARC Launch Training Manual, p. 13.

they are: not interested, would like to speak with the pastor further concerning the future church, or they are ready to join right now with no further persuasion. From these interest meetings, a group is established that will eventually launch a church. This group may be augmented by a strong mother church that has sent several people to move with the launch team and the planter to the city of the new church. Summit Church in North Carolina attempts to get people to move to the cities where they are planting new churches to assist the planter and the launch teams.[25]

Further training continues until the launch day. Massive amounts of digital and print marketing (mail-outs) are used to invite the local community to the launch day. As the launch date approaches, the planter will begin to lead the launch team through their first version of a "Next Step" program (membership, discipleship and involvement training). By the time the launch day has arrived, the team will have already had one to four practice or preview services where they will attempt to work the bugs out of the service and location venue. At launch, the church may already have some part-time staff in place to help with administration, and the goal will be to (ideally) attract several hundred people to the launch day. If the launch day is very successful, the new church may potentially attract several hundred people on day one. Usually, over the course of the next month or so, this number decreases to its lowest average attendance. (Hopefully, this number is 50-60% of the launch day number). A major goal of the large launch model is to break the 100 or 200 church barrier goal from day one. If a church can do this, its chances of long term success and viability are very good.

---

[25] Stetzer, Ed. 2019. "Finding the right Church Plant Model: The Traditional Model (Part 2)." Edstetzer.com, January 3, 2019. Accessed February 22, 2019. https://edstetzer.com/2019/01/finding-the-right-church-plant-model-the-traditional-model-part-2/?mc_cid=6d4694e95f&mc_eid=0f447d78ed

Strengths of the Large Launch Model:
-may break the 100 attendee barrier from day one
-increased long term success rate
-financial viability sooner than the traditional model
-finances may provide for limited staffing
from the start or soon after the start

Weaknesses of the Large Launch Model:
-this model requires large amounts of initial funding
-usually requires extensive training for the church planter
-sometimes not as successful in large, urban environments
-often other churches are not planted from these churches
-an event-based, possibly entertainment model may not create discipleship in some of the non-engaged participants

4.4 Missional Incarnational/Emergent Church Planting

seeks to be the hands and feet of Jesus embodied in the flesh. These churches desire to be on mission for Christ in all they say and do. The Missional Incarnational Church stresses more on who the people are rather than calling themselves the church when they meet together.

Missional churches are not always small but may tend to be smaller as they generally are more concerned with discipleship than numerical church growth. Missional Churches tend to be more concerned with the Kingdom of God expressing itself in practical ways than with large buildings or traditional church norms. Missional Incarnational Churches are also known to rely heavily on the concept of community. Communities do not normally function around a centralized leader, but more often kind-of coexist with several leaders. In "Starting Missional Churches," Nick Warnes presents the idea that the church with a charismatic pastor personality at the center often does well in the initial stages, but if the pastor exits the situation, it is like a spider's head being cut off, and the entire organization may die. However, when a starfish loses an arm (plural leadership), the animal just keeps right on going.[26] Stetzer describes these churches as having four characteristics: "1) They desire to incarnate in the community 2) They are highly relational 3) They engage in holistic mission, and 4) They disciple their way into a church".[27]

Missional Churches often look very dissimilar to traditional churches. Some "Missional" pastors have been given the pastorates of traditional churches where they have taken out the pews and replaced them with tables and chairs in order to facilitate discussion around a table in the place of the traditional worship experience, which many think of when they consider "having church."

Missional churches may meet in coffee houses, restaurants, and some even meet in bars. The missional approach to church has much more to do with discipleship than any of the things that revolve around traditional church experiences (buildings, ecclesiastical hierarchy, church budgets, youth and children's programs, etc).

In the circles that the author runs in, these are possibly the most controversial churches. Some believe that they are not to be considered churches at all. On the other side of the fence, those in missional churches, criticize the traditional church for its many failings. While the missional church may not look much at all like the traditional church, it should be commended for its desire to produce disciples. "The hope is that church planting can be a more common expression

---

[26] Mark Branson, and Nicholas Warnes, *Starting Missional Churches* (Downers Grove, Illinois: Intervarsity Press, 2014), 25.

[27] Stetzer, Ed. 2019. "Finding the right Church Plant Model Part 4: The Missional Incarnational Approach." Edstetzer.com, January 9, 2019. Accessed February 22, 2019.https://edstetzer.com/2019/01/finding-the-right-church-planting-model-part-4-the-missional-incarnational-approach/

of discipleship in the lives of everyday people in everyday churches in America."[28]

Strengths of the Missional Incarnational Model:
-known to be very relational
-discipleship is stressed and valued
-approach is to change the person, outer community and world

Weaknesses of the Missional Incarnational Model:
-this model sometimes speaks against and downplays the role of the traditional church
-service and social justice may trump Gospel teaching and preaching
-sometimes missional communities get off track theologically as they stress community and may neglect sound doctrine

4.5 House/Simple/Organic Churches

are the next type of church planting model. Sometimes they are referred to as house church because they meet in a house. Sometimes they are referred to as simple church because they value minimal structures and programs. Sometimes they are referred to as organic because organic has little extra and unneeded/un-natural ingredients added. All three terms can often be used interchangeably. The house/organic/simple church movements have a number of different faces, but most house church movements have some similarities. House churches have probably been most successful in China. China has five major house church movements. Most of China's Christians attend, were baptized in, and are discipled in house churches. The country has five major house church movements: China for Christ, China

---

[28] Mark Branson, and Nicholas Warnes, *Starting Missional Churches* (Downers Grove, Illinois: Intervarsity Press, 2014), 32.

Gospel Fellowship, Yin Shang Church, Li Xin Church and Word of Life Church.[29]

While these movements all differ somewhat in theology and practice, four out of five have been identified as either Pentecostal or Charismatic. The last group, Word of Life Church, has been described as similar to Southern Baptists in theology. While the range of theology and expression of worship is varying, many methods are similar. All five groups fall into the house church model. In 2002 over 53 million Chinese Christians were of the Charismatic or Pentecostal persuasion alone.[30] These organic groups often lack the formality and structure of what most Americans think of as "church," but they have been highly successful in training believers and reproducing themselves. In America, groups are attempting to copy this approach, but they do not seem to be catching on with much of the success of the Chinese. There are two distinctive traits that seem to characterize the Chinese house church movement. One of the traits is that they are Pentecostal or charismatic and the other trait is that they experience severe persecution. Four out of five of the main house church movements are charismatic, and this can be modeled in this country. At the same time, all five of the major movements are experiencing a very large degree of persecution. At least at this moment, the American church is not experiencing severe persecution. However, one wonders if persecution is a requirement for the kind of growth both the early Church and now the Chinese church are experiencing.

---

[29] Wesley, Luke, "Is the Chinese Church Predominantly Pentecostal?" (Asian Journal of Pentecostal Studies, Vol 7, Issue 2, July 2004): 242. Accessed November 20, 2018. http://web.b.ebscohost.com/ehost/pdfviewer/pdfviewer?vid=4&sid=-30ca5f3c-1f0f-430a-962b-c7bacb702445%40sessionmgr104.

[30] Wesley, Luke, "Is the Chinese Church Predominantly Pentecostal?" (Asian Journal of Pentecostal Studies, Vol 7, Issue 2, July 2004): 227. Accessed November 20, 2018. http://web.b.ebscohost.com/ehost/pdfviewer/pdfviewer?vid=4&sid=-30ca5f3c-1f0f-430a-962b-c7bacb702445%40sessionmgr104.

Ed Stetzer notes that house churches seem to do best in restricted areas (persecution), but also on college campuses, large apartment complexes, and expensive urban/high-density cities.[31]

Also, people who are disenfranchised, weary, or intimidated by the more institutional and organized forms of the church may be open to an Organic Church.

Downsides to the house church planting model, include the collection of funds to pay a manager or central leader. Since this is an organic model, it may take a lot of time in order for enough of these churches to exist to funnel enough money to the instigator of the group to become fully funded by these churches tithes or associational dues. This does not present a problem for most house church planters who already were gainfully employed in their city or community before starting a house church movement. If someone was to go into a large city or another geographic region with the idea of starting a house church movement, however, then they may need financial backing from an outside organization for several years while the group gets off the ground.

Others have noted that house churches are difficult to control. Walter Brown, in a review of the book Home Cell Groups and House Churches by Kirk Hadaway, Francis Dubose and Stuart Wright, notes that while it may be true that it can be difficult to control house churches and cell groups, "(1) it is easy to keep forgetting that vital, meaningful ministry and worship cannot really be controlled, that following the Spirit's leadership is risky, that God is ever more than He is known to be (2) if cell group and house church work were

---

[31] Stetzer, Ed. 2019. "Finding the right Church Plant Model Part 5: The Organic House Church Model." Edstetzer.com, January 16, 2019. Accessed February 27, 2019. https://edstetzer.com/2019/01/finding-the-right-church-planting-model-part-5-the-organic-house-church-approach/?mc_cid=5cce7f1c8b&mc_eid=0f-447d78ed

programmed until all the unknowns were eliminated, it would be nothing more than a reproduction of the structure and programming which sent the people looking for something different and more vital in the first place."[32]

Strengths of the House/Simple/Organic Model:
-financial demands are low
-discipleship is stressed
-ministry fulfillment is easily accessible to most who are interested in being involved
-reproduction may be more easily scalable than complex models like the large launch

Weaknesses of the House/Simple/Organic Model:
-ministry may be low quality (example - preaching and music)
-house churches (because of their very nature) are difficult to control

4.6 Multi-site or Campus Churches

are the last type of churches. Multi-site churches are very popular in America today, with many churches choosing to open more branches of the main church rather than attempt to build forever larger buildings on one site. What many people consider to be America's largest and second-largest churches are both multi-site churches. While the trend for the megachurches of the 1980s and 1990s was often to build arena and stadium size behemoth buildings, some of them closed down, and others were forever hindered by the monumental debt associated with building an auditorium that seated 5,000-10,000

---

[32] Walter E. Brown, review *Home Cell Groups and House Churches*, by Dubose, Francis, The Theological Educator, 41 Spring (1990), pp. 203-206, accessed February 27, 2019.

people in some cases. The young associate and youth pastors of these megachurches (the next generation of megachurch pastors) witnessed this. For many of them, it would become more attractive to start one church in many locations.

These models often involve video broadcasts of the main pastor to satellite locations around their city, and today, even around their state or for some, the entire country. When looking at almost any list of the largest churches in America in 2019, it is very difficult to find two lists that agree. Some of the confusion is that the vast majority of megachurches now have several locations. What would once have been considered to be small denominations are now considered one church. Because of the sharing of resources, these churches are often easier to start since they have a lower start-up cost. "One church in several locations" can share the same pastoral staff, office staff, maintenance staff, and church accounting software. Bob Hyatt of Evergreen Community Church in Portland, Oregon, says, "[Multisite] give us the benefits of a church plant without most of the risks."[33]

While multi-site campuses have many proponents, there are also those who believe it is not the best idea. In 2014, Pastor Mark Driscoll resigned from his then powerful "Mars Hill Church." His board was quoted as saying, "Driscoll is guilty of 'arrogance, responding to conflict with a quick temper and harsh speech, and leading the staff and elders in a domineering manner.'"[34] When Driscoll resigned, he was pastoring an empire of churches that all watched him on video weekly. Within just a few months after the pastor's resignation, the

---

[33] Hyatt, Bob, abstract article "Under Discussion", Christianity Today, Vol. 53 Issue 10 (October 2009), p. 12.

[34] Burke, Daniel, "Mark Driscoll, top megachurch pastor, resigns", Newspaper Source Plus, CNN Wire, October 15, 2014: 227. Accessed March 25, 2019. http://web.a.ebscohost.com/ehost/detail/detail?vid=9&sid=b15ecb53-98cd-4b1d-a282-309f41d15926%40sdc-v-sessmgr03&bdata=JnNpdGU9ZWhvc3QtbGl2ZQ%3d%3d#AN=BAQ41413407195&db=n5h

entire church and its campuses collapsed. Other detractors of multi-site churches lodge complaints about the need for one pastor to be the communicator when qualified associates abound. "…And why show a pastor on the screen yet have a campus pastor? Is the campus pastor not fit to teach? If he is, then why is he not teaching?"[35]

Strengths of the Multi-site or Campus Church Model:
-financial demands are low in comparison with starting a new church from scratch due to sharing of resources
-a reproducible, high quality, worship service experience is already produced

Weaknesses of the Multi-site or Campus Church Model:
-ministry and leadership of multiple locations may be dependent on only one senior pastor
-associate and campus pastors may be stunted in their growth due to lack of preaching and teaching experience

---

[35] White, Thomas, abstract article "Under Discussion", Christianity Today, Vol. 53 Issue 10 (October 2009), p. 12.

CHAPTER 5

FIVE FACTS ABOUT CHINESE HOUSE CHURCHES

House Churches: Breaking the Secret Chinese Formula of Success

House churches are a phenomenon in China. They have transformed the Christian experience in the country with the largest population on the planet. Because of the proliferation of house churches in China, Luke Wesley, said in the Asian Journal of Pentecostal Studies, that "If trends…remain constant, by 2020; there will be more evangelical Christians in China than in any other country in the world."[36] Many denominational and associational groups in America have decided to copy the model in America. While this model can work anywhere, it is important to notice that there are several factors in China, especially during the years of explosive house church growth that are unique to China as opposed to America.

It is also helpful to understand something about the difference in officially sanctioned Chinese churches, which are called Three-Self

---

[36] Wesley, 226.

Patriotic Movement Churches (TSPM) and house churches. Chinese House Churches operate outside of government blessing, sanctioning, or control. For a time, these churches were completely outlawed and driven underground (which only fueled their growth). Today it is often not the case that the unsanctioned church is underground, but they are a completely different type of organization than TSPM churches. TSPM churches deal with several government-imposed laws that the house churches object to. Some house church leaders may feel that TSPM church leaders have compromised in some areas while other house church leaders completely denounce TSPM churches as "atheists" churches that are not a part of the Body of Christ. The second group of leaders described who are completely against TSPM churches, have arguments which may be summed up in several points. TSPM churches are required to comply with the following unbiblical regulations: 1) government registration of the churches' meeting location, time and leader 2) registered leaders must have a seminary education approved by the atheistic government 3) churches must agree to not spread the Gospel to or baptize anyone under the age of eighteen 4) churches are not permitted to pray for the sick or drive out demons 5) churches may not welcome traveling preachers and 6) churches may not communicate with foreign churches or their branches.[37] While there are many obvious problems with the Chinese government's regulations that are listed above, two are possibly the most glaring. When you 1) do not allow children or teens to join the church, you severely stunt its growth, and 2) when only certain people are allowed to lead existing churches, it is almost

---

[37] Anonymous house church member author, "Differences Between House Churches and Three-Self Churches" (Chinese Law & Government, 2017, Vol. 49, Issue 3), pp.161-163. As accessed from Business Source Complete Database, through the Harold Hunter Theological Library, Ebscohost, Accessed November 20, 2018.

impossible to start new branches of the church. The Chinese government hates one Christian principle above all others, the priesthood of believers. When any government gets involved, the Church is frequently transformed into a place where it is more," Institution than fellowship, more formality than family and, a church which placed clergy above laity."[38] When a government stops people from hearing from God to lay hands on the sick, disciple new believers, or start new churches, they have crippled the movement. In Christianity, it is our God-given right to hear directly from God and do His will to create good change in the world.

When considering Chinese churches, it is good to realize that many churches probably characterized as "house" churches are not always small, and many are not in houses at all. A big distinction in China is more along the lines of registered or unregistered churches. In fact, in 2019, a church that had 50,000 attendees and a very large building to match, was demolished by the Chinese government. This church certainly would fit the characteristics of a "house" church, but none the less, it was unregistered, so the government tore it down. In this case, the government used explosives and excavators to destroy the building of the "Golden Lampstand Church" in Linfen, Shanxi, China.[39]

It is important to note several facts about Chinese house churches that are very, very different from many American churches.

---

[38] Brown, Walter, "Home Cell Groups and House Churches" (The Theological Educator, 41 Spring 1990), p.204. As accessed from ATLA Religion Database, through the Harold Hunter Theological Library, Ebscohost, Accessed November 20, 2018.

[39] Ireland, Michael, "'Chinese Authorities Blow Up Popular Megachurch", Charisma News, March 8, 2019; accessed May 10, 2019, https://www.charismanews.com/world/75499-chinese-authorities-blow-up-popular-megachurch

5.1 Fact #1- Chinese house churches have experienced major and serious persecution for years

"Sister D," who was one of the leaders of China for Christ Network during its formative years, notes that the organization became Pentecostal while it was "quite isolated and experienced considerable persecution."[40]

In America, some groups have attempted to replicate the numerical success of Chinese house churches, but without the severe persecution. We may speak of "light persecution" when we are actually discussing someone speaking negatively about us or calling us bigots because we said the Bible calls homosexuality a sin, but this is NOT strong persecution. While I do not necessarily pray for persecution for myself or any others, severe persecution and a cultural backlash against promoting Christianity are two very different things. One lady in a house church in China that is called "D," went to prison for the cause of Christ. She was asked if she was mistreated in prison? Her answer was, "Yes, they beat me," she continued to explain that "The prison officials tried to prevent her from preaching or praying: they beat her and shocked her with an electric baton on the chest. In spite of these difficulties, she was able to minister to many in prison."[41] This account lines up with many, if not most Chinese house church leaders who are often imprisoned, kidnapped or killed for the cause of Christ. For many, it is considered the norm to be imprisoned for the cause of Christ. House Church leader, Peter Xu, concerning persecution, said, "Some died for the sake of the Lord; some were imprisoned; some escaped from China; some compromised their faith in fear; some betrayed the Lord and friends. Few dared to openly

---

[40] Wesley, 232.
[41] Wesley, 237.

confess that Jesus is Savior."⁴² Chinese house churches are different in several ways from many American churches, but in this respect, they are different from all American churches as of 2019.

The concept of persecution is not just an accepted fact among house church leaders. It is considered by some as key component and needed doctrine which God uses to build the church. If the component is not present, then the house church leaders may feel that they are missing a part of the ministry of Jesus. House churches are on a mission for Jesus and take this very seriously. They expect opposition to their ministry. "House churches assume the grand mission of the Bible as their responsibility and must at all times succor souls from evil and lead them to God."⁴³ The mission of saving souls must not just be fulfilled, but many leaders believe it must be fulfilled in a manner that emulates the work of the Lord.

> *"If it were not for the work done by the Lord, no one would risk death to spread the Gospel; it is to bear testimony about the Gospel that Jesus' followers martyr themselves. Hence they felt no shame in suffering persecution in the name of Jesus. That is the path of the cross indicated by Jesus, and the path that must be taken to rise to heaven."*⁴⁴ *-The words of an anonymous house Chinese Church leader.*

While American Christians are now beginning to experience light persecution in the form of possibly losing their business for refusing to serve people whose lifestyles their consciences will not allow

---

⁴² Xin, Yalin, "Inner Dynamics of the Chinese house church movement: the case of the Word of Life community" (Mission Studies, 25, no 2, 2008), p. 161. Accessed November 20, 2018.

⁴³ Anonymous, 165.

⁴⁴ Anonymous, 166.

them to support, we are still in stark contrast to the past and current realities of house church and non-registered church persecution in China. Chinese pastors and leaders are frequently jailed or simply disappear. With stakes, these high, possible Chinese house converts are sure to have counted the cost before being baptized, starting a new church, or baptizing someone else. If the stakes were this high in America, the Church would look radically different than it does today.

5.2 Fact #2- Chinese house churches are most frequently Pentecostal and/or Charismatic in nature, relying heavily on the supernatural with obvious manifestation of spiritual gifts as the norm, not the exception

Unlike many American church plants which often seem to rely more heavily on strategy and marketing, Chinese house churches often have a "strong emphasis on the miraculous, with prayer for healing taking on an important role in the life of faith".[45]

These characteristics of healing and miracles correlate naturally with the Pentecostal and Charismatic affinity of the house church movements that are predominant in China. Luke Wesley notes that "China for Christ Network is widely recognized as the largest house church group in China" and that they have a "Classical Pentecostal orientation."[46]

In America, Pentecostal and Charismatic churches have a very large presence, especially in the South, but we are still smaller than mainline, Baptist churches, and many non-charismatic, independent churches. While worldwide in the early 2000s, there were "Over 200 million denominational Pentecostals and over 500 million

---

[45] Wesley, 226.
[46] Wesley, 232.

charismatics and Pentecostals around the world"[47], in America, Pentecostals and Charismatics are still sometimes excluded as legitimate and treated as second class Church citizens when it comes to being included in some Church circles. Highly eloquent, respected, and educated scholars like Dr. Jack Hayford, have broken the mold in some cases, but for the most part, the tongue talking and miracle expecting Christians have been pushed to the sidelines of the American Academic religious conversation. In China, this is just the opposite.

In China, the vast majority of Christians are Pentecostal or Charismatic. Both groups practice speaking in tongues, with the only major distinction being that "Pentecostals" often hold to the fact that tongues are the "initial [or first] evidence of Holy Spirit baptism" while Charismatics may not make this distinction, but still practice speaking in tongues or at least heavily affirm all the gifts and Biblical manifestations of the Spirit as being in operation for today. After a scholarly analysis of Chinese Christians, Luke Wesley, in the Asian Journal of Pentecostal Studies, concluded that, "Study suggests that 90% of house church Christians and perhaps 80% of the total Christian population in China would affirm that the gifts of the Spirit listed in 1 Corinthians 12:8-10 are available to the church today".[48]

In China, Christians often do not have the luxury of considering the quality of the youth and children's program at one church as opposed to the church down the street. The question is not "Did the parking lot teams have Disneyland style golf cart trams to shuttle us into the building or were we forced to walk over 400 feet?" Rarely has a Chinese Christian chosen their church based on music style or the decibel level of that music. In China, the questions more often revolve around subjects like, "Will I be imprisoned if the service is interrupted by the government tonight?". The pastor's wife may need

---

[47] Wesley, 249.
[48] Wesley, 243.

to ask, "Will I be able to sustain myself if my husband is imprisoned for several years or if he is executed?" In these circumstances, books being written about whether or not the gifts of the Spirit are for today would be ludicrous. In this context, the church NEEDS and DEPENDS on the power of God for today, simply to survive.

From this place of persecution, the dependence on the Spirit flows. The Chinese House Church movement exhibits the following three characteristics: "1) A strong emphasis on personal experience…2) A strong expectation that God will intervene in miraculous ways…3) A strong sense of their own weaknesses and dependence upon God."[49]

5.3 Fact #3- Super successful Chinese house churches participated in a form of multi-level marketing type training for new believers and leaders

Chinese house churches quickly reproduce leaders that are capable of teaching others the fundamentals of their new faith. This system is often so refined and structured in some of the groups that it very much resembles multi-level marketing with American product companies like Amway, Avon, or Herbalife. Many of the great success stories of American multilevel marketing companies have very little to do with the quality of the product. What makes multi-level marketing successful is that the people involved, get more people involved in the products which then find more people to get involved. Most of the time, a successful multi-level marketing company has streamlined and refined their speeches and techniques (example - the way a product party, like Tupperware is to be executed in such a way as to have the highest possible impact.) In many or most Chinese house church movements, there is similarly a very defined system of 1) evangelizing 2) recruiting 3) discipling 4) training and 5) reproducing

---

[49] Wesley, 244.

more believers in a way that is similar to the large refined multi-level marketing techniques.

In many American churches, we have a very limited system of systematic discipleship. In some ways, American churches treat new converts as if the churches' only job is that of the evangelist. In other words, many pastors and churches do lead people to faith in the Lord, but then everything after that decision seems to be left to chance. Jesus told us in the great commission that we are to make disciples, not just count "decisions for Christ." *"Therefore go and make disciples of all nations, baptizing them in the name of the Father and of the Son and of the Holy Spirit, and teaching them to obey everything I have commanded you. And surely I am with you always, to the very end of the age."* **Matthew 28:19,20 NIV.**

Chinese house churches often go to great lengths to ensure that their new believers are well equipped to be successful disciples of Christ. While many American churches do have small groups or Sunday School classes, a much lower percentage of churches have a clearly defined process to move people from a decision to follow Christ to becoming a well-equipped believer who is ready to defend their faith and to share it with others. While most growing and large American churches do have "Next Step" or "Growth Track" classes that accomplish this well or at least partially accomplish this, the system in many Chinese house church movements is much better defined and refined.

The Word of Life House Church Movement, which grew to more than an estimated 20 million Christians in less than 50 years, has a very well-crafted training and discipleship system. Word of Life converts are taught seven principles that laid out the basics of the Christian life. These principles are not a 45-minute class that claims to then have people know enough to be set for life. They are, "...Principles of spiritual practice for Christian believers, a basic curriculum for training workers, and guidelines for Bible Study and the ministry of the church…It includes twenty-one lessons in three units (over 100 pages)."[50] The Word of Life Church has an expectation of how someone enters and moves through their process of initial discipleship. The process is as follows: 1) frontier evangelism 2) people coming to faith in Christ 3) going through Life/Truth meetings 4) believers responding in faith 5) receiving TE (theological education) training and 6) joining the Gospel band.[51] This process involves initially attending an evangelism meeting, which may last for three days or so, followed by attending a "Life" meeting that seeks to answer the major questions of life, like, "What happens when we die?". The "Truth" meetings, which can last for as much as 7-15 days, teach basic truths of discipleship. When someone completes the Life and Truth meetings, they can then attend "TE" or Theological Education; this process is 40 days. Then a leader may choose to attend TE 2 which is a six-month course that covers most of the Bible. If the church recognizes someone who is a high capacity leader, they may send them to TE 3 which is formal seminary education, which may actually be overseas.[52]

This process combined with the leadership structure of the Word of Life Church completely sets the movement apart from 99% of American churches where in contrast if you get saved, you may be asked to simply become a member in a church service, possibly attend a simple membership class or even in more organized systems, you may likely only attend 3-4 hours of training before you are considered a good, participating member in some of America's largest churches. This rapid discipleship process means that many new believers could go from a new convert to a reasonably well-trained

---

[50] Xin, 162.
[51] Xin, 172.
[52] Xin, 169-172.

believer, equipped to teach others in less than six months. "While it normally requires three to four years to train a pastor in the west, it only takes six months of intensive underground seminary training to produce a house church pastor. The explosive growth of the WOL house church network is greatly aided by its speedy turnout of workers into ministry."[53]

In American circles of the 1970s through the 1980s, some Pentecostal/Charismatic flavored house churches were very much opposed to hierarchies within their organizations and believed they were called to restore the "Kingdom" not to build local church buildings into denominations. One of these groups even had the catchphrase of "The abomination of the denomination."[54] This revolutionary approach may sound catchy to the young, but possibly in part due to its lack of organization, the historians of this movement considered it mainly dead by the 1990s. In contrast, while Chinese house churches may not have a lot of impressive buildings or high compensation for even some of its most prominent leaders, the leading Chinese house organizations were and are in no way opposed to highly organized systems and structures to maintain fellowship, accountability and mutual encouragement. This system may even give prospective leaders a clear vision of the group of leadership that can be aspired through attending the various trainings and leadership mentorship possibilities.

As would be expected from the type of efficiency observed in the new believer's discipleship method of the Word of Life group, they also had a similarly well-oiled leadership connection paradigm. In

---

[53] Xin, 180,181.

[54] Percy, Martyn, "Restoring the Kingdom: the radical Christianity of the house church movement" (Journal of Contemporary Religion, 14 no 1 Jan 1999), pp. 157-160. Harold Hunter Theological Library, ATLA Religion Database, Accessed November 20, 2018.

the initial "Seven Principles," one of the principles that were taught is "Interlink and Fellowship." From the start, the church plants ideas in the new members that it is good and necessary to stay connected with other branches of the movement. The lowest level of the church is the house church, raising up through a total of six levels to its highest level of "Connection and interlink" in the General Conference. The levels are house church, coworkers meeting, area coworker's meeting, pastoral districts, pastoral regions, and general conference.[55] The church meets in at least four types of meetings to facilitate its purposes and to maintain the interlink and connection. The four types of meetings are: 1) regular meetings [worship, Bible study, prayer meetings, testimony meetings, hymns and praises, Sunday School and youth meetings] 2) spiritual formation meetings [evangelistic meeting, revival meeting, truth meeting, thanksgiving and solemn meeting] 3) holy occasion meetings [baptism, communion, wedding, birth and funerals] and 4) coworkers meeting [area coworkers meeting, regional coworkers meeting, area representatives meeting, regional representatives meeting and general conference].[56] In the Word of Life Church (and most other Chinese house church movements), very little is left to chance in the way of discipleship and leadership development and connection. They have taken the mandate to "make disciples" very seriously.

5.4 Fact #4- The Mega Success of Chinese house churches occurred and occurs primarily in rural areas

As someone who has recently traveled constantly in the United States (over 45,000 miles via motorhome, 3,000 air miles, about 2,000 miles via train, 1,500 via car and a few hundred by bicycle in about 18

---

[55] Xin, 169.
[56] Xin, 175.

months), to more than 100 churches, I can say with assurance that cities and rural settings have entirely different views on the world. The rural/urban differences permeate people's thinking, the way they worship, the use of their time, the expectations they hold of churches and church services, and possibly even what motivates them. City people are in no way superior or more important than country folks; however, they are two very unique and different cultures that complicate things in another way when it comes to duplicating what happened in Chinese house church origins.

Some churches that I attend in the country are relatively isolated from other churches that are similar in theology and similar denominational backgrounds. For this reason, the lack of competition allows for sometimes flourishing ministry paradigms in the country that may not even work in the city. In cities, worship wars seem in full swing in 2019. It is common to go to even small-city churches where seemingly every week, the worship leader adds a new song to the mix, and if the praise and worship content is more than three years old, a great sin has happened. In rural settings, there are often very strong churches that are considered contemporary in the sense that they utilize "praise and worship" music, but the music they utilize is often 10-20 years old. This seems to be no deterrent to many rural congregations that very much enjoy these songs of praise from the 2000s, or even the 1990s and 1980s. In doctrinally similar urban churches, while this may be the case from time to time, it would seem much less prevalent that a contemporary church would not be cutting edge in the music style.

Other differences can be seen where customs and traditions of 20-40 years in most city churches that have faltered greatly, still flourish in many country churches. For example, Sunday evening services and Sunday School have normally fallen out of favor in cities being replaced with small groups or in the case of Sunday night services, nothing at all. In the country, this often is not the case. In rural settings, such as Empire Pentecostal Holiness Church in Cochran, GA, the church has maintained a Sunday School attendance which is often more than 80% of the morning worship attendance and the Sunday and Wednesday evening worship service attendance, while not as impressive as Sunday School stats, it still remain very viable and reasonable services with many people in the congregation still attending regularly. Some urban churchgoers may be tempted to attack Empire PH Church for its lack of "cutting edge" ministry, but the church plays an important role in its denomination as a consistent giver to missions and as a community of believers in the Cochran, Georgia area. Empire has many committed believers who attend faithfully up to five and six services per week between Sunday School, Morning Service, Evening Service, Wednesday service, prayer meetings, men's and women's meetings, and other service projects and events. This kind of behavior is rarely seen by city church attendees who are possibly more distracted with long commutes, a host of school-related children's and youth activities, high-pressure job demands and a litany of other events and distractions which are amplified in a large, urban environment. Three authors recognized in 1987 that house churches and their close cousin, home cell groups, may assist in city environments with spreading the Gospel because of: "(1) unbelievers' growing resistance to the gospel...(2)the churches' persistence in using traditional structures in diverse urban settings *[which are not being effective]*[57]* and (3) the growing trend in home-related Christian life and ministry on a broader scale..."[58]

The very successful Chinese house churches (for the most part) originated in rural or extremely rural environments.

---

[57] *explanatory note added by Brian Farley
[58] Brown, 203.

> "The WOL church represents a community of rural house churches in China, although its evangelistic ministry has no doubt touched a significant portion of the urban population as well. Rural populations are considered to be 'the poor of the marginalized' in China, in their economic, educational, and political status. And Henan Province, where the WOL movement originated, is considered the marginal of the marginal among China's 23 provinces. So, effective ministry among the poor is no doubt one of the essential elements of the dynamic growth of the WOL movement."[59]

These rural house churches became so prevalent that with time, many rural residents moved to cities, taking the house church movement with them. Some have noted that what worked incredibly well for the house churches growth in the country did not always translate well in urban environments. While many believe the greatest difference among Chinese churches is between the house church movement and the Three-Self Patriotic Movement (TSPM), which is the official state-sponsored and sanctioned church, some have seen the divide between city and country churches in China as even greater. In his book, *House Church Christianity in China: From Rural Preachers to City Pastors,* Lie Kang sees a significant difference in the two. "Kang's analysis places a more significant division on the rural/urban rather than house church/TSPM."[60]

In the modern Chinese city environment, King even notes that in cities, some house churches in the city of Linyi, China, "Are very

---

[59] Xin, 176.

[60] White, Chris, "House Church Christianity in China: From Rural Preachers to City Pastors" book review, (Studies in World Christianity, 23 no 2, 2017), p. 188-189. Harold Hunter Theological Library, Ebscohost, Accessed November 20, 2018.

public in their meetings, even with signs or neon crosses to mark their meeting points"[61] while a few decades ago this would have been unheard of. While this sounds very promising, there are also very recent reports in the news of Chinese non-registered church buildings being demolished by the government.

> "The Golden Lampstand Church in the city of Linfen, northern Shanxi province, was destroyed on Sunday using dynamite and heavy ...The church was purportedly built with almost £2million raised by local worshippers. A Catholic church in the neighbouring province of Shaanxi was also reportedly demolished last month, 20 years after it opened. There are 60million Christians in China."[62]

5.5 Fact #5- Chinese house church movements were started by deeply committed men and women of God who burned with passion for the Lord and called others to wake from their spiritual stupor

While today, many American churches seem to be very concerned with not offending anyone, seeker-sensitive or partially seeker-sensitive approaches, Chinese house church movements that spread quickly like wildfire were not started in ways that took people's feelings into

---

[61] White, 189.
[62] Connor, Neil, "Christians outraged as China destroys mega-church", Daily Telegraph (London). 01/12/2018, p16-16. Harold Hunter Theological Library, Ebscohost, Accessed March 28, 2018. http://web.b.ebscohost.com/ehost/detail/detail?vid=5&sid=b5b19815-faa4-45ba-bf0d-138014111a0f%40p-dc-v-sessmgr03&bdata=JnNpdGU9ZWhvc3QtbGl2ZQ%3d%3d#db=n-5h&AN=8Q2133481005

much consideration. Chinese house churches were started from a place of power, desperation and fervent evangelism.

Speaking of Peter Xu (founder of the Word of Life Movement [WOL]), the house churches he planted were described as the "furnace" of evangelism, which spread quickly from place to place.[63] During these initial years, "The preaching and teaching of this period of time focused on the theme of salvation through the cross, how to reject evil and live a new life in Christ, necessity to suffer and witness for the Lord, and some basic doctrinal truth."[64] Concerning some of the initial meetings of the WOL, Peter Xu's fervor for the Lord was so powerful that, "twenty to thirty people walked together [*following Peter*] from meeting to meeting....When brothers and sisters heard that Peter Xu had just arrived, they quickly spread the news and people started to come in hundreds".[65] In explaining his early methods, Peter said, "For example, when they felt the love of God and their own sinful nature, we reminded them of the work of Christ on the cross and declared to them God's forgiveness of sins."[66] Peter preached for "13 consecutive days and nights...Every day there were several scores to over a hundred people being baptized."[67]

Chinese house churches were started in a spirit and mode of revival and desperation. People were reminded quickly and plainly of their plight of being sinners in need of the forgiveness of God. The founders of these organizations were often not rewarded with large suburban homes with a Lexus in the driveway but were often rewarded by imprisonment. While no one except God knows another man's motivation, it would appear that a divine and immediate sense

---

[63] Xin, 165.
[64] Xin, 165.
[65] Xin, 166.
[66] Xin, 166.
[67] Xin, 166.

of urgency to "snatch them from the fire" permeated almost every decision in church planting and evangelism made by the leaders of WOL and others Chinese house church movements. In America, many good, godly and respected megachurch pastors could be described as experiencing great wealth, vacation homes, family bonding on many pleasant vacations, being chased by Christian magazines for interviews, becoming somewhat famous as Christian television stars, and being blessed financially in many ways by the Lord. In contrast, Peter Xu and many others like him have ministries described in a way similar to the following, "In the 40 years or so of ministry, he experienced homelessness, separation from his family, was chased, arrested, beaten and imprisoned by the authorities, suffering in many ways for the Lord. And yet he felt privileged to be called of God to ministry and was willing to suffer for his faith."[68]

Modern technology, knowing your audience, advertising techniques, and social media should not be discounted as worthless or some betrayal of the Gospel. At the same time, if we are to attempt to copy the success of Chinese house churches in America, we must realize that the WOL was not started with flashy marketing, lighting, bass subwoofers, cool instagram pics or other trendy techniques. When you look at large launch/attractional churches of today, there are very few similarities to these organizations and the house churches of Asia from the 1960s to the 1990s. One of the few places where there may be an overlap is the efficiency of the House Churches to train and mentor new leaders with the fast-growing American churches which employ a growth track strategy to quickly get people involved in ministry. Outside of this, very few other similarities are noticeable.

---

[68] Xin, 167.

CHAPTER 6

DENOMINATIONAL MODELS AND APPROACHES SAMPLER

America and the world are full of a variety of denominations and church movements. Each has their own unique approach, flavor, success or failure rate, average size, and doctrinal peculiarities. In this section, we will delve into several denominations and groups to consider some of their church planting thoughts and experiences. Groups will include Assembly of God, Southern Baptist, Episcopal, Anabaptist (Mennonite), and American Baptist.

6.1 Anabaptist/Mennonite/Brethren Church

The Anabaptist Church which has morphed into what we now call Mennonites (with varying internal groups having both conservative/liberal stances) and Brethren in Christ Churches, not only can be found driving horse and buggies, like their Amish cousins, but contemporary Mennonites are involved in all forms of church ministry. From the most conservative churches imaginable to seeker-sensitive and attractional models of church planting, Anabaptist has a full spectrum of church cultures represented. In his article, "Church Planting: An Anabaptist Model," Dale Stoffer (a Brethren Church

Historical Scholar at Ashland University) set forth much more of a theology to be preserved rather than practical insights and strategies of modern church-planting techniques. Stoffer argued that many or most current Anabaptist groups were not interested in preserving their form of church, but were far too concerned with numbers and church growth over the preservation of the Anabaptist doctrine and distinctive traditions. Stoffer explains that Anabaptist doctrine is not to be preserved for the sake of preserving a denomination, but instead, these doctrines should be preserved because they are biblical, not simply because they are anabaptist.

Stoffer stresses that principles (normative truth derived from Scriptures) are to be preserved while forms (external expressions which principles take in a given time and culture) can change with the times. In the author's view, the Anabaptist church can leave forms (externals), but cannot lose the principles.[69] Stoffer makes the case that Anabaptist Churches should stick to their theological and doctrinal roots even if they change the form and exterior look of their worship services. Dr. Stoffer offers a theological basis for Anabaptist Church planting that he maintains can build a strong church fellowship.

Anabaptist Churches have a very different view of the "Church" than most protestant denominations. Anabaptists believe in believer's baptism and the believer's church. The Anabaptist view of the Church presented by Stoffer can be summed up with four points: 1) the Church is a community 2) the Church is to be visible 3) the Church is composed of the disciples of Christ and 4) the Church is gathered and led by the Spirit.[70] This is an oversimplification, but basically, the Mennonites believe that the Church is dependent on each

---

[69] Stoffer, Dale R., "Church Planting: An Anabaptist Model", Brethren Life and Thought, 39, no 3, Summer 1994, p. 210. Harold Hunter Theological Library, Ebscohost, Accessed December 5, 2018.

[70] Stoffer, 212-213.

other, the clergy, and the laity. The Church only consists of those who are actively living out their faith in Christ through Christlikeness, servanthood and the active leading of the Spirit. The namesake of the Mennonite Church, Menno Simons, described the "Marks of the true church of Christians be known. Menno's list includes pure doctrine, scriptural use of the ordinances of baptism and Lord's Supper, obedience to the Word of God, unfeigned brotherly love, open confession of Christ and God, and suffering for the sake of the Word of the Lord."[71]

Dr. Stoffer contends that the Anabaptist movement as a whole requires much out of their adherents and this commitment level should be used as a biblical, practical tool in order to build a new church community. The old idea is that if you ask little of people you will receive little, and if you ask much of people, then you will receive much. Stoffer mentions the contrast between Anabaptist and other churches to explain that in Anabaptist tradition, it requires the entire church to fulfill its role. The Mennonite church is required to be fully involved in the ministry of the Gospel in order to fulfill its purpose; other protestant churches only need to preach the Gospel and administer the sacraments to fulfill their purpose as a true church. "In contrast to the Lutheran and Reformed marks, which can be accomplished by the clergy with little involvement from the laity, the majority of marks in both Anabaptist lists can be effectively accomplished only by the believing community."[72] "For the Anabaptist, the church is not optional. It is an integral part of God's eternal plan to form a people for himself."[73]

The Anabaptist model should not give in to the seeker-sensitive or "need-oriented mode" of the church. Stoffer believes that the

---

[71] Stoffer, 214.
[72] Stoffer, 214.
[73] Stoffer, 215.

seeker-sensitive movements teach "Only a thin veneer of the gospel… baptizing people not into radical discipleship to Christ but into a faith heavily accommodated to modern culture.[74]" Anabaptist faith teaches a strong concept of discipleship with personal accountability, and watering down the message leads to a church that is no longer Anabaptist at all, in Stoffer's view, not Biblical. An example cited is the Mennonite core conviction to nonviolence and pacifism (conscientious war objection and other violence objection). Those in the Anabaptist camp who disagree with Stoffer, believe that the commitment to nonviolence (in all forms), "…Gets in the way of evangelism and church growth, and consequently, they should be minimized so as not to offend."[75] Stoffer "violently" disagrees with disavowing non-violence (and further abandoning the doctrinal peculiarity of the Mennonites in general) that he suggests baptismal vows should include, "…The willingness to both give and receive counsel that a statement on discipline should be included in the constitution and by-laws of new congregations. If a church does not begin with a commitment to accountability and discipline, it will be difficult to arrive at one later."[76]

The Anabaptist model of church planting suggested, is a unique model in American society, but one with much merit. He reminds church planters that obedience to Christ, selfless service, practical, daily Christian living, and leading by the Holy Spirit are all essentials in order to start a church that will fulfill its Biblical mandate. While Stoffer's model deals almost exclusively with doctrine and religious philosophy, at the conclusion of his paper, he does offer a few pragmatic and practical points for church planters, that may be helpful regardless of one's theological leanings. Stoffer suggests making

---

[74] Stoffer, 216.
[75] Stoffer, 217.
[76] Stoffer, 218.

small groups a part of all new churches as groups allow for: leadership formation, discipleship, and fellowship. Stoffer notes that most Anabaptist churches never grow to more than 150 because they are so reliant on fellowship (as an Anabaptist character trait) that the 150 number is the highest a large, small group can grow to realistically. Small groups offer an opportunity for fellowship to be maintained outside of the normal worship services. Additionally, Anabaptist churches are encouraged to immediately emphasize and practice shared ministry, the priesthood of all believers, and outreach. "In addition, a church which is more concerned about self-preservation rather than outreach through evangelism and social concern will be a dying church."[77]

The Anabaptist tradition of high commitment and responsibility among its members has much in common with Wesleyan/holiness theology; perhaps it is time for many new churches and their movements to reacquaint its potential and new members with the fundamentals of the faith and its practical commitments which have helped these churches continue for centuries. A great lesson that can be taken away from the Anabaptist model of church planting presented here, is summed up in Stoffer's closing thought, "Though commitment to these principles may make church planting in the Anabaptist more difficult, faithfulness to Christ and our own heritage should cause us to follow the way of radical obedience to our Lord rather than the way that is touted as easier or more likely to succeed."[78]

6.2 An Episcopal Church Planting Perspective

In 2006, Susan Brown Snook set out to plant a church in Scottsdale, Arizona. An article she wrote titled "Reaching New People through

---

[77] Stoffer, 219.
[78] Stoffer, 220.

Church Planting" describes the story of the Church of the Nativity and has a few insights from Episcopal church leaders concerning church planting.

In 2006, Bishop Kirk Smith of the Episcopal Diocese of Arizona, set out to plant 10 new churches in his territory. Church of the Nativity in Scottsdale, AZ, was one of them. Nativity started with, "Fourteen people meeting in a living room, over the next few months, we continued to meet for prayer, Bible study, and visioning about the church we dreamed of planting. The committed core invited others to join our adventure, and our group of fourteen quickly grew to sixty-five enthusiastic members."[79] Snook credits the growth (which would transition from meeting in an elementary school to becoming a church of 250 members in three years time with its on permanent meeting space, a staff of six and a budget of $300,000) to asking three questions: "Who are we? Who are our neighbors? and Who is God calling us to become?"[80].

In 2001, the Episcopal Church published, "New Church Development: A Research Report," this paper found seven factors that correlated with the success of new Episcopal Churches. Success, for the purpose of this report, is defined as achieving financial self-sufficiency within seven years. The factors that the report identified include: 1) careful site selection 2) a community context where the population is well-educated and relatively affluent 3) effective recruitment and training of lay leaders 4) shared vision and direction 5) a young minister who is good at starting groups from "scratch" 6) a

---

[79] Snook, Susan Brown, "Reaching New People through Church Planting". Anglican Theological Review, 92, no 1, Winter 2010, p 111. ATLA Religion Database, as accessed from the Harold Hunter Theological Library, November 18, 2018.
[80] Snook, 112.

focus on reaching unchurched community residents and 7) systematic efforts to track visitors and prospects.[81]

Often when people think of the Episcopal Church, one would imagine educated, affluent people. This report reveals that this would not be by accident as the Episcopal Church encourages its church planters to seek out well-educated and relatively affluent communities. The Church of the Nativity certainly fits this exact mold, but Susan Brown Snook does note in her article that "success" should not just be defined as financial self-sufficiency, but should be defined as well by evangelistic and practical ministry metrics. During the time that Scottsdale Nativity was planted, other Arizona church plants were also established that included a Sudanese congregation, a Spanish-Speaking congregation, and a congregation aimed at at-risk youth. These congregations were not considered to meet the "success" requirement of the Episcopal Church but were still important none-the-less.[82]

According to the Episcopal Churches' own research, it is experiencing a significant decline. When Bishop Kirk Smith became bishop of Arizona, "The decade of the 1990s had seen Arizona's population grow by 40 percent-yet no new churches had been planted, and average attendance had remained flat. His vision of ten new churches in ten years aimed to help the Episcopal Church in Arizona make up for lost time".[83] This type of vision is needed in the Episcopal Church in general if things are ever to be turned around. A "State of the Church" report from 2009, showed a decline in worship attendance from 2003 to 2007 of 10.5% and a loss of 148,197 active members

---

[81] C. Kirk Hadaway and Penny L. Marler, "New Church Development: A Research Report" (New York: Episcopal Church Center, 2001), p 4-5; as accessed April 17, 2019 www.episcopalchurch.org/files/ncdreport2.pdf
[82] Snook, 114.
[83] Snook, 112.

during the same time frame.[84] While many evangelical conservatives will contribute this to the continually left-leaning, liberal policies and doctrines of the Episcopal Church, Snook attributes it to the age of the Episcopal church. While the situation may not seem to be as severe on the surface for some evangelical groups, all churches, conservative or liberal, Evangelical or Ecumenical, must face the reality that if we do not start more churches than we close, we face a losing proposition.

6.3 An Evolving United Methodist Church

In 1990, Adam Hamilton founded the United Methodist Church of the Resurrection in Leawood, Kansas. The Church of the Resurrection was founded in a funeral home with about 100 people at its first service, growing within two years into a local elementary school. By 2001, the church had a 1,700 seat sanctuary, 8,800 members, and a weekly attendance of more than 5,500 people. From the beginning, the church was not ashamed of being a part of the United Methodist Church (UMC) and prominently displayed UMC logos and church literature.[85]

The United Methodist Church, as a whole, is not growing; in fact, it is in steady decline and has been for an extended period of time. A 2006 article cited UMC figures showing that in 2004, the United Methodist Church was down .81 percent, which brought them to slightly more than 8 million members with an attendance decline of

---

[84] House of Deputies Committee on the State of the Church, Report to the 76th General Convention (2009), p 75, as accessed April 17, 2019. https://extranet.generalconvention.org/staff/files/download/364.pdf

[85] Dart, John, "Proud of the UMC Label", The Christian Century, 118, no 25, September 12-19, 2001, p. 12. Harold Hunter Theological Library, Ebscohost, Accessed December 5, 2018.

.96 percent.[86] This figure does not sound that bad until one considers that the UMC has been in decline for at least 36 straight years as of 2006. This decline has continued in recent years. The official United Methodist statistical data website, UMData.org, recorded under its most recent "stats" page that total membership was 6,806,331 as accessed on April 19, 2019.[87] Since the 2006 article referencing 2004 numbers only used the wording "slightly more than 8 million", we do not have an exact count, but in approximately the last 15 years, the UMC has lost at least 1,193,669 members. To put that into perspective, the Church of God, Cleveland, Tennessee, one of the countries largest Pentecostal denominations, showed a membership of 1,189,304 in the entire United States and Canada as of 2011.[88] It would take a complete removal of every single Church of God member in the United States and Canada, and every one of those churches to be closed simultaneously to have the same effect as the number of members that the United Methodist has lost in the last 15 years or so.

While the reasons for such drastic decline among mainline American churches are surely complex and multifaceted, a great debate continues to rage as to how much of this decline is associated with the LGBTQ agenda and whether a church is welcoming or affirming of alternate lifestyles. Esther Chung writes in March of 2018 that "'Reconciling' United Methodist Churches Lose Members." A group inside the UMC called Reconciling Ministries Network

---

[86] Christian Century, "Methodist Ranks Drop for 36th Straight Year", Vol. 123, Issue 10, p15. May 16, 2006, accessed April 19, 2019.

[87] UMData.org, "UMData, the United Methodist Church Online Directory and Statistics", General Council on Finance and Administration of the United Methodist Church, 2019; accessed April 19, 2019, "Stats" link, http://www.umdata.org/UMFactsHome.aspx

[88] Church of God International Offices, Church of God 74th General Assembly Minutes (Cleveland, TN: Pathway Press, 2012), 18.

(RMN) was founded in 1982 to "advocate for the gay community."[89] Using data from UMDATA.org, Chung debunks a popular argument from RMN and others who defend churches that officially adopt LGBTQ affirming status. Chung explains that RMN claims that when churches officially adopt an LGBTQ affirming status that, yes, their membership and attendance may initially drop, but within a relatively short period of time, it will rebound with those who appreciate this theological posture.

Chung explains that RMN claims a "V" shaped data curve; that is when the church becomes RMN affiliated, it will initially suffer a drop in both membership and attendance, but it will quickly rebound. Chung's research showed that this is only true long-term about 10% of the time. The other 90% of RMN affirming congregations lose members and attendance in the short term and the long term. Among the UMC's five American jurisdictions, the smallest average decline of membership reported after becoming a "Reconciling" congregation by Chung was 5.74%, and the largest was 11.57%. Across those same jurisdictions of the church, the lowest average attendance decrease was 3.75%, but the largest average attendance decrease was 21.29%. Chung stresses that the results of local congregations, without averages of an entire group of churches mixed in, can be much more devastating. For example, upon becoming a "Reconciling Congregation," Good Samaritan UMC of the California-Nevada District claimed over 400 members and 207 average worship attendees. Over the next five years from 2011-2016, the church "grew" to 357 members and 135 in attendance. Considering for the viability of a church, attendance is often much more important than membership as it is the

---

[89] Chung, Esther, "'Reconciling' United Methodist Churches Lose Members", Juicy Ecumenism: The Institute on Religion and Democracy's Blog, March 28, 2018; accessed April 20, 2019, https://juicyecumenism.com/2018/03/28/rmn-causes-decline-united-methodist-umc-congregation/

average attendees who are committed enough to pay the bills, in this case, the Good Samaritan Congregation was left with only 65% of its original attending congregation. Chung explains that this dramatic case is common among many RMN churches "with only a handful of exceptions."[90] Liberal critics of Chung, immediately point out that the UMC is declining as a whole. Others respond that is it possible that the UMC's decline as a whole can at least, in part, be connected to the RMN and other similar forces. While the overall reasons for UMC decline can be debated, it would certainly appear from Chung's research that the RMN at least plays a part in the narrative of the UMC's decline.

In this United Methodist environment, it is interesting that Adam Hamilton's United Methodist Church of the Resurrection grew to become the largest UMC in America over the last 30 years. For the first four years of Church of the Resurrection's growth, Adam Hamilton personally delivered a church coffee mug to over 900 people who had visited the church.[91] While it is highly unlikely that Hamilton still does this as Church of the Resurrection is now the largest UMC in America, other things have changed as well.

> *"Hamilton said for the first 10 years he led Church of the Resurrection in Leawood, Kansas (the UMC's largest church), he would have considered himself a "traditionalist," which is a person who welcomes same-gender attracted people, yet believes that same-gender relationships do not fall in God's will. However, more recently*

---

[90] Chung.
[91] Dart, 12.

> *Hamilton has changed his view on the topic—more appropriately, his view of Scripture has changed.*"[92]

Like many church leaders, Hamilton has changed his stance on homosexuality, and more importantly on his view of scripture. In a November 2018 article by Juicy Ecumenism: The Institute on Religion and Democracy's Blog, 25 growing United Methodist Churches over 1,000 people showed that, "Evangelicals Once Again Dominate List of Top-growing Large UM Congregations" suggesting that remaining Biblically true, is not only good spiritually, but Biblical orthodoxy is also good for the numerical growth of local churches.[93] Like many modern megachurches, the theology that built their churches is not considered enough to sustain it. It will be interesting to see, in the years to come, if we are given this time before the imminent return of Christ, how Church of the Resurrection will do in terms of membership and attendance.

6.4 The Southern Baptist Convention

For many years the Southern Baptist Convention (SBC) has held the claim of being the largest Protestant denomination in America with over fifteen million members and a peak American membership of 16.3 million in 2003. Unfortunately, in June of 2017, *Christianity Today* reported that the SBC had lost 78,000 members in the prior

---

[92] Briggs, Megan, "How Progressives View Scripture (and Homosexuality in the Bible)", August 6, 2018, Church Leaders.com, accessed April 19, 2019, https://churchleaders.com/news/330294-homosexuality-in-the-bible-adam-hamilton-progressive-view.html.

[93] Moran, Dan "Evangelicals Once Again Dominate List of Top-growing Large UM Congregations", Juicy Ecumenism: The Institute on Religion and Democracy's Blog, November 20, 2018; accessed April 22, 2019, https://juicyecumenism.com/2018/11/20/evangelicals-dominate-list-top-growing-large-um-congregations/

year, had the lowest baptism count since 1946, the lowest membership since 1990, and the lowest worship attendance since 1996.[94]

Some Southern Baptist leaders blame, "The downward trajectory on their struggle for effective evangelism," but politics professor George Hawley at the University of Alabama has suggested that the decline can be linked to, "the Religious Right" when during the presidential election of 2016, SBC leaders split over support for Donald Trump.[95] Many SBC leaders have hoped that conservative theology would stop the SBC from a decline in the face of so many mainline churches declining over recent LGBQT battles, but acclaimed SBC Scholar and Missiologist Ed Stetzer notes that "Southern Baptists are shrinking faster than United Methodists."[96]

In 2016, the only metric in which the SBC was growing was new churches, "Adding 479 churches…for a total of more than 47,000."[97] While the growth rate of SBC churches is somewhat encouraging, the total picture of the statistics suggests that there will not be enough people to fill those churches if current trends prevail. This great giant of a church finds itself struggling to turn the tide of the last three decades of decline. The same *Christianity Today* article reporting these SBC statistics, closed by adding that while the SBC had been declining for years, "the Assemblies of God, America's third-largest denomination, enjoyed domestic and global growth."[98]

---

[94] Shellnutt, Kate, "Hundreds of New Churches Not Enough to Satisfy Southern Baptists", Christianity Today, June 9, 2017; accessed April 19, 2019, p 2, https://www.christianitytoday.com/news/2017/june/southern-baptist-convention-churches-baptisms-sbc-acp.html

[95] Shellnutt, 4-5.

[96] Shellnutt, 3.

[97] Shellnutt, 2.

[98] Shellutt, 4.

6.5 The Growing Assemblies of God

In the January 2017 article, "AG Reaches Historic Number of New Churches," the denomination reported that "The U.S. Assemblies of God closed 2016 with the highest annual number of new churches in its history. The 406 new churches also bring the total number of U.S. churches to 13,023-exceeding the 13,000 mark for the first time".[99] The Assemblies of God seems to have bucked the trend of most denominations in America. Perhaps this is in part because of a dedication to conservative theology, combined with reaching and becoming, "Increasingly diverse with 43% of adherents being non-white ethnic minority" in harmony with the model they have adopted of "Matching Fund Churches" from their Church Multiplication Network.

In this model (which was made popular by the Association of Related Churches [ARC] and is now being emulated by wise groups across the country), a planter raises up to $30,000, and the denomination matches that amount. The successful church will then pay that back over time until the initial investment is returned. The funds are exclusively used to fund another church plant, so these funds become perpetual and ensure a pool of resources to equip future church plants and planters. This system is very similar, if not identical to the ARC system of funding with the exception that ARC may match up to $50,000-70,000 in some cases.

This model has produced a more than 90% five years survivability rate among these new Assembly of God Churches, and 17% of current Assembly of God Churches (as of January 2017) were launched during the eight-year time frame that the Assembly of God Church

---

[99] Forrester, Mark, "AG Reaches Historic Number of New Churches", Springfield, MO: General Council of the Assemblies of God, 2017; as accessed April 19, 2019, p. 2, https://news.ag.org/news/ag-reaches-historic-number-of-new-churches

Multiplication Network has existed.[100] Whatever the reasons for this success, it is obvious that the Assemblies are being blessed by God while so many movements are struggling. The Assemblies are also experiencing global growth with, "Nearly 68 million AG adherents in over 365,000 churches throughout the world."[101] Hopefully, other denominations, movements, and associations are taking note and will also emulate this funding process which, combined with a strong vetting component of potential planters, seems to frequently produce viable churches. While ARC numbers are often much higher, the Church Multiplication Network of the Assemblies of God currently reports that the average church in their network has an attendance of 81.[102] This number is well on the way to the "magic" 100 number that many have identified as a number needed to sustain a church with financial solvency past the five-year mark. The current Assemblies of God Church Multiplication Network model seems to be serving the AG very well.

---

[100] Forrester, 2.

[101] Forrester, 3.

[102] Assemblies of God. "AG Trust Assemblies of God." agtrust.org. https://agtrust.org/Initiatives (accessed April 19, 2019).

PART III

THE CHURCH PLANT STUDY, MISSIONAL/EMERGENT CHURCHES, URBAN PLANTING & BREAKING BARRIERS FOR SMALL CHURCHES.

CHAPTER 7

THE CHURCH PLANT SURVIVABILITY STUDY OF 2007

The *Research Report: A Publication of the Center for Missional Research, North American Mission Board - Church Plant Survivability and Health Study 2007* contains extremely valuable church planting insights from one of the largest church plant studies in recent years. The study followed 2,266 separate new church plants from several denominations. Over the course of four years, the study researched results from these churches which hailed from: Southern Baptists, Sovereign Grace Ministries, Baptist General Convention, Leadership Network, General Baptists, Wesleyan, New Thing Network, Assemblies of God, Evangelical Free, Foursquare, Christian Church and Lutheran Church Missouri Synod. Ethnically, the poll surveyed churches representing 57% Anglo, 17% Hispanic, 5% African American, 6% multi-ethnic, and 15% among a variety of other language groups.[103] Over the course of the study, these churches

---

[103] Stetzer, Ed and Connor, Philip, *RESEARCH REPORT A Publication of the Center for Missional Research, North American Mission Board,* Center for Missional Research, 2007, accessed November 18, 2018, p 1. https://pcamna.org/churchplanting/documents/CPMainReport.pdf

averaged about 43 people in their first year and grew to an average of around 84 people by year four.[104]

The report is over forty pages long, here I attempt to simplify some of it and in just a few pages, highlight some of the report's extremely helpful findings. Church Plant Survivability and Health Study Key Findings include information about the following: attendance and baptisms, factors associated with higher attendance and baptism counts, best facilities to use, average funding, average receipts, church planter work levels, self sufficiency rates, four factors associated with church plant survivability, church plant health/growth and subsequent baptism rates, four more factors associated with church plant attendances and three more factors associated with baptisms.

7.1 Factors Associated with higher Attendance and Baptism Counts:

New churches that tract like the normative church in this study can expect a first-year attendance of 42 growing to 84 by year four. Average baptisms for new churches grew from ten in year one to 14 by year four.[105] The report lists many factors that are associated with higher church attendance. Those factors assisting church attendance include: meeting in a school or theater, conducting special children's events like egg hunts and fall festivals, using mass mail to invite people to services, conducting new member classes, using a signed church covenant, starting at least one daughter church within three years of planting, having a stewardship plan which helps the church move toward self-sufficient status, having several staff members at the start of the plant as opposed to a single staff member, paying the church planter, providing health insurance to

---

[104] Stetzer and Connor, 2.
[105] Stetzer and Connor, 2 and 4.

the planter, conducting block party outreach events, delegating leadership roles to church members, conducting leadership training for church members, planter works full-time as opposed to part-time or half-time, being assessed as a planter before choosing a church planter and having the church planter's expectations realized.[106] The factors involved in increasing higher baptism counts were: engaging in ministry evangelism such as food banks and drug/alcohol recovery programs, starting at least one daughter church in three years, having a proactive stewardship plan to become self-supporting, conducting mid-week children's programs, conducting children's special events, sending out mailers, conducting a block party, conducting new member classes, conducting leadership training for church members, the planter receiving church planting training in a boot camp or basic training style, working full time as the church planter, being assessed prior to the church planting process and delegating leadership roles to church members.[107] While both of these lists are important, it should be noted how many of the same things appear on both lists, so these should have special attention paid to them. One observation of these lists is that the larger and more complex of systems the planter puts in place in the formative months before and after launch, seem to increase the likely hood of a large congregation. To have more staff, stewardship systems, new membership classes and member leadership training are all complicated systems, but all seem to assist with reaching more people with the Good News.

7.2 First Year Insights

While the first few years of a churches' existence are extremely important for setting the outlook for the years to come, the study shows

---

[106] Stetzer and Connor, 3.
[107] Stetzer and Connor, 5.

that nothing compares to the vitally important first year on a statistical basis. The study showed that the average new church grows by about 77% on average in year one, this number decreases yearly, plaining out on year four at around a 15% attendance growth.[108] While it is true that percentages are difficult to maintain even if you are truly growing (example - growing from 10 to 18 is an 80% growth rate; growing from 100 to 118 is only an 18% growth rate and to grow a group of 100 by 80% requires a new number of 180), still the first year sometimes sets the tone for the years to come. Likewise, baptism count per 100 members, is also very important in year one. On average, year one baptisms average 30, with that number declining to about 17 by year four.[109] It is important to do everything possible to see year one succeed. The first year of a new church plant is often its most productive year for many years to come.

7.3 Facilities Insights

Facilities also play an important role in church planting according to the report. The report lists seven possible meeting places for new churches. These include schools, theaters, church buildings, homes, business establishments, hotel conference rooms, and community halls. The report breaks down those churches which use a certain type of facility in year one and what percentage of churches continued to use these facilities over the next four years. Breaking these into three categories, we can see a trend. The first category are facilities that people use less statistically from year one to year four. The places that people used less were: homes and hotel conference rooms. The places that people used the same level percentage-wise through the four years were schools and theaters. The places that people used

---

[108] Stetzer and Connor, 15.
[109] Stetzer and Connor, 16.

more over the course of the four years were: church buildings, business establishments, and community halls. These trends suggest that schools, theaters, church buildings, business establishments, and community halls may be better places to start larger churches than houses and hotel conference rooms.[110] While church buildings are obviously very convenient to hold services in, they are often not available to a new church plant. Theaters and schools are convenient due to size, built-in seating and they often have stage areas. As a church planter who met in a hotel conference room for several months, and then was able to move to a small church building, I can testify that a hotel conference room often "smacks" of this is a temporary group that is not going to make it. The moment a new church plant can move into a church building, it often gives at least a small amount of credibility from the moment you are there. For the church we successfully started, it sent the message that "Hey, at least these people have a little church building now, maybe they will make it."

7.4 Funding, Planter Compensation/ Benefits and Church Receipts

The study monitored new plant funding, planter compensation, and average receipts. The average church in the study received approximately $34,000 of first-year funding, $27,500 in year two, $20,000 in year three and $19,700 in the fourth year. Using an inflation calculator, in the year 2019 dollars, this year 2006 numbers from the study would mean the average church today might expect to receive $42,871 in the initial year, $34,675 for the second year, $25,218 in year three and $24,840 in year four. Two factors connected to funding proved to be good predictors of church size and success rate. These factors were church planter compensation and medical insurance.

---

[110] Stetzer and Connor, 7.

The more the planter can be compensated, the greater the churches' chance of success.

Ninety percent of church planters in the study were employed full-time (more than 40 hours per week) in the process of starting the church.[111] The compensation and full-time status of the church planter appears on both the list, which is associated with higher attendance and the list for higher baptism counts. This indicates that the more time the planter can put into working for the church, the greater the likelihood that the church will survive. When it comes to the church planter's compensation, the survive-ability report also dived into providing medical insurance for the church planter. Those denominations and sponsoring churches that provided medical insurance for the planter saw an average of about thirteen more people attending the church in its initial year (about 35 for those churches without medical insurance for the pastor to about 48 people in attendance for those churches providing medical insurance). This gap becomes greater as the formative years pass with year four averaging about 73 for those churches without medical insurance to an average attendance of around 104 for those with insurance.[112] This is of special note since many church planting experts believe that more than 100 people attending is a church planting sweet spot for long-term congregational survivability.

When considering funding, as the church grows, more and more funding will hopefully come from the new congregation itself. The average church in the study took in around $38,000 in year one and increased to about $92,000 by year four.[113] In the year 2019 numbers, this year 2006 statistics, equal about $47,915 in year one to $116,004 in year four.

---

[111] Stetzer and Connor, 11.

[112] Stetzer and Connor, 39.

[113] Stetzer and Connor, 10.

While it seems obvious that a new church will need a lot of funding, what is counter-intuitive, is that as the new church grows, they will need more and not less money. The above new church receipts numbers would appear to indicate that a new church will need little to no support from outside sources by year four, but it is important to remember that, "The more a new church succeeds, the more likely it runs the risk of financial shortfalls."[114] Since new churches are frequently more fruitful than established, older congregations, it is not rare for a denominational church plant to quickly outgrow the size of the churches which are sponsoring them. The sponsoring churches or organizations may often be made up of pastors who weekly lead 75-100 people. When they hear that the new plant is running 150, 200 or 300, they may tend to think that it is time to quit pouring funds into these groups; however, it will take much more money to keep these new churches afloat. When considering that it often takes several years for a new believer to work their way into tithing, it is often the case that the church growth is the main thing actually working against the finances of the new church. With church growth, new demands for larger buildings, staff teams and resources of every kind emerge. Church planting agencies often ignore this dynamic and remove funding too quickly. For this reason, if the planter can think ahead enough to keep a cushion of funds, it will be to their advantage. It will be to the denominations advantage to continue funding for four to five years. Many planters do not talk about finances until it is too late, and those who steward large amounts of finances faithfully are often turned off by being pressured to bail the church out of this or that financial crisis.

Jesus spoke of the need for financial planning in Luke..."Suppose one of you wants to build a tower. Won't you first sit down and

---

[114] Jim Griffith and Bill Easum, Ten Most Common Mistakes Made by New Church Starts (St. Louis, MO: Chalice Press, 2008), Kindle Location 683.

estimate the cost to see if you have enough money to complete it?" **Luke 14:28 NIV**

The study also followed the self-sufficiency patterns of new churches that survived for five years, that is to say, when a church no longer needed outside funding. In the first year, only 30% of new churches were self-sufficient. By year two, the number increased to about 41%. In year three, about 54% of churches were self-sufficient. Year four showed around 63% of churches were self-supporting, and by year five, 70% of churches in the study were self-sufficient.[115] These numbers would seem to indicate that the longer a denomination, association or sponsoring church can assist the new church, the more likely the new church is of being able to make it long term since each year that the church exists, the higher the self-sufficiency rate increases. In other words, from a purely financial basis, if outside funding were stopped in year one, seven out of ten new churches would fail, but if funding were stopped in year five, only three out of ten new churches would fail.

7.5 Four Factors Associated with Church Plant Higher Attendances

The study showed that four factors were reflective of the churches' attendance being higher. These factors are: new membership classes, using a church covenant, church reproduction, and medical insurance for the pastor.[116]

Attendance factor one = New Member Classes

New member classes help churches assimilate new people faster and therefore increase attendance. In year one, those not having

---

[115] Stetzer and Connor, 12.
[116] Stetzer and Connor, 38-39.

a new member class had an average attendance of about 27 while those with a class had around 44. The impact of this classes' presence or absence is much more pronounced in year four when the average church without a class had 51 in attendance, and the average church with a class had 95.[117] Today, these classes are often a part of a "Growth Track" which is an extended session of classes ranging from membership, to personal discipleship, to "dream team" membership (personal ministry involvement). The numbers are clear that some type of official process to get people involved in the church systematically is very important, causing the churches that do so to be almost twice as successful as those that do not by year four.

Attendance factor two = Church Covenant Use

Connected closely to the New Member Class is the Church Covenant Use. At the end of the New Member Class, prospective members are asked to sign a "Church Covenant." The covenant normally is less than a page long and asks the members at a minimum to commit their life to Jesus and their attendance, finances, and participation to the church. These covenants can be very simple, in the case of many attractional churches, to rather complex in the case of other churches. The point is that the new members should stop and consider what they are doing when they join the church. This increases new church attendance. Year one averages for those churches that did not use a covenant were about 31 attendees and those with church covenants were about 44 attendees. Unlike new member classes, this distinction of using a covenant or not seems to be less significant with time, as in year four, those churches without a covenant averaged about 82, and those with a covenant averaged about 87.[118]

---

[117] Stetzer and Connor, 38.
[118] Stetzer and Connor, 38.

Attendance factor three = Church Reproduction

Church reproduction also had an impact on the new churches' attendance. Churches that planted a daughter church within three years averaged 51 in year one as opposed to about 38 in those that did not. These same churches had a dramatic difference in attendance by year four when they averaged about 130, while the churches that did not plant another church averaged around 75.[119] One could argue that a church must be larger and stronger to plant a daughter church in the first place, but some have made a commitment to plant other churches even if their current church is not very strong. What is certain is that since the average church which planted a daughter church was only running about 130 in year four, is it that these were not churches that were running 1,000 that could "afford" to seed off 30-40 people or so. Starting a daughter church will always require a sacrifice of some level, but the stats show that this is a good sacrifice. Just as a mother experiences incredible pain and adjustment to produce a new child, the joy far outweighs the pain. Additionally, one could argue that the young female grows in all sorts of ways when they have a child. Similarly, the new church plant who plants early, plants from a place of youthful energy. Life produces life, and it is often healthiest and less risky for a female to reproduce earlier in life rather than late in life. The same could be said for churches.

Attendance factor four = Medical Insurance for the Planting Pastor

Medical insurance for the planter has already been discussed in conjunction with church planter general compensation. It plays a significant role in the higher attendance numbers. Year one, 35 people without it, opposed to 48 with insurance for the pastor. Year four

---

[119] Stetzer and Connor, 39.

shows, 73 without a medically insured pastor and 105 with an insured pastor.[120] Perhaps the pastor can stay healthier by going to the doctor more frequently without major concern? The pastor who misses less days from work due to sickness can reach a few more people for Jesus in the first year and a lot more people in year four.

7.6 Four Factors Associated with Church Plant Survivability

The study researched over 100 factors that may account for new church survivability or failure. Four factors stood out as especially significant. The factors are: Church Planter Expectations, Church Member Leadership Development, Church Planter Peer Group, and Stewardship Plan.[121] The good news concerning these factors is that every one of them are controllable factors.

Survivability factor one = Church Plant/Planter Expectations

The first factor is Church Plant/Planter Expectations. If the church planter had their expectations met, the chances of church plant survival increased by over 400%. Eighty-seven percent of those church planters whose expectations became a reality had a church which survived. Only 61% of churches whose planters' expectations were not met, had surviving churches.[122] There is a place I call "Ministry Dream World." Almost 30 years ago, I started as a volunteer youth pastor at the age of 16 in a small church and then started officially preaching at age 18. At that time, because of my youthfulness, pride and ignorance, I just knew that if I ever started a church, it would have thousands of people the first year, it would probably be the largest in the city by year two and probably we would need a civic center

---

[120] Stetzer and Connor, 39.
[121] Stetzer and Connor, 14.
[122] Stetzer and Connor, 14.

type building or so to hold the mammoth crowds by year three. Now that is a little bit of an exaggeration, but I certainly had expectations that did not match reality, even though I was relatively "successful" early on in ministry. After years of discussion with ministry peers, I have found that many pastors (especially younger ones) have these similar thoughts. This is a special place in the mind of young ministers; we call "Ministry Dream World." It is similar to "Fantasy Land" at Disney World. It's the place where magic happens every day, everyone is happy, the forest is enchanted, and the seven dwarves whistle while they work. "Ministry Dream World" is similar - magic happens every day, everyone is happy, the soundboard and lights always work properly, all children's church and nursery volunteers show up early and are happily excited to minister to the hundreds of kids in the back, our musicians could all be easily qualified to play with the Philharmonic Orchestra or Phil Collins, but they are simultaneously as spiritual as a group of foreign missionaries to third world countries, the new church board members are all high-level leaders of Fortune 500 companies, but respect the pastor and church simultaneously and would never cause a problem, and the greatest problem the church has is figuring out where to park all 5,000 attendees that attend the perfectly administered 8, 9:30 and 11:15 a.m. services. In Ministry Dream World, most of these problems all happened in less than six months of the churches' existence.

The problem with ministry dream world is that often the reality is less like Fantasy Land and more similar to the chills of the Haunted Mansion and attendance can often drop as fast as the Tower of Terror descends from high heights to low lows causing that stomach being thrown to the top of your head feeling. The study suggests that the church planter's expectations being met are what is important for the long term survivability of the new plant. For some, who may naturally be very humble and possibly have lower expectations, these expectations may need to be stretched to ensure that the church reaches its greatest potential in the formative years. For those who may live in a ministry dream world though, the team who initially vets the planter before they are chosen should probably talk through what church planting success normally looks like. For every mega-church there are hundreds, if not thousands of regular churches, and for every new church that is running 500 in less than a year, there are hundreds, if not thousands, who do not run 50 in a decade.

This is not meant to be discouraging or faith dampening, only to encourage planters to have realistic expectations. God can do anything, but if we plan to be faithful even if the thing He is doing is seemingly small, then there is a greater chance He will reward largely in the future. If the planter is not faithful with the small, there is no promise of the large.

Survivability factor two = Church Member Leadership Development

The next major factor of church survivability is Church Member Leadership Development. Developing leaders for church growth is a two-way street. Every church that grows, must have more qualified leaders to operate, maintain and grow ministries. These ministries thus produce more opportunities for more new people to become assimilated into the life of the church. On the flip side, most people will not stay in a church if they are not involved. The more talent, energy, skills, and intellect a person has, the less likely they are to come to church only to sit on a pew. People want to use their talents and gifting, and if they are not challenged and growing, then they are much more likely to leave and find a church where they will be put to good use. Churches that have an effective Member Leadership

Development Plan increase their chances of survival by more than 250%.[123]

Survivability factor three = Church Planter Peer Groups

Church Planter Peer Groups are the next factor that determines long-term church survivability. If the planter feels alone and out of fellowship, then chances are greater that they will quit. A peer group of planters can lift each other up and encourage one another when times get hard. Many denominational groups and associations have realized this, and some now start several churches in different parts of the same city simultaneously with the plan of interacting with each other from day one. Pastors in general, often feel isolated and can be prone toward depression; this is magnified with church planting. As a church planter, one often moves to a new city with no friends and a very limited network and fellowship opportunities in that city. These peer groups can also serve as fertile ground for exchanging of city-specific ideas of what is and is not working among the new churches and launch teams. The more a planter can stay connected to a group of peers for networking, encouragement, and accountability - the greater the plant's likelihood of success - the success rate increased 135%.[124]

Survivability factor four = Stewardship Plan

The last factor is Stewardship Plan. While all churches should have a plan to teach members stewardship principles, for new churches, this is especially important. The study shows that if a church has a plan to move the church toward financial self-sufficiency, this

---

[123] Stetzer and Connor, 14.
[124] Stetzer and Connor, 14.

"Increases the odds of survivability by over 178 percent".[125] Most old churches with debt-free facilities and lots of senior adults with large chunks of disposable income can cruise for years with little to no vision, administration or stewardship plans. The work was done long ago, teaching people to tithe, give to missions and meet yearly financial promises. New churches have a very small window to get people giving. If this does not happen very rapidly, the new church is almost destined for failure. While the new church may grow in attendance, if it is not also growing in finances and personal financial stewardship responsibility of its newly assimilated members then it is destined to fail. Each year, less and less support comes in from outside sources and the new church is obligated and responsible to pay the bills somehow. This is why it is important to teach stewardship from the very beginning to both increase the likelihood of the new churches' existence as well as to increase the financial blessing and financial IQ of those who attend the new fellowship. The later these stewardship principles are taught, the more likely the church is to financially fail.

---

[125] Stetzer and Connor, 14.

CHAPTER 8

Arguments Against the Missional and Emergent Church Movements

8.1 Missional and Emergent Church Movements

Missional Churches are churches that tend to stress the church doing social ministries and "being on a mission" in the community. The term "Emerging Church" may be more familiar to some in the church circles. "Emerging" or "Emergent Church" is sometimes interchanged for "Missional Incarnational" Church communities. "Today's 'emerging church' [is] another label applicable to some of the missional communities."[126] The Emerging Church and Missional Incarnational Churches are not always the same thing. Some Missional Incarnational Churches are of very conservative theology. While theology in the "Missional Incarnational" church camp maybe liberal or conservative, most of

---

[126] Effa, Allan, "Pub congregations, coffee house communities, tall steeple churches, and sacred space: The missional church movement and architecture", Article, Missiology, 43 no 4 Oct 2015, p.376. Harold Hunter Theological Library, Ebscohost, Accessed November 18, 2018.

the theology of the Emerging Church Camp holds a low view of the scripture and a high view of service to others. People who may not consider themselves theologically liberal or "emergent" in theology do have things in common with the Emerging Church, regardless. Most members of the larger Missional Incarnational community movement agree with the Emerging Church movement that radical change is needed in the traditional church world. These churches concentrate on the community. Missional Incarnational churches often meet in non-traditional buildings such as restaurants, pubs, or apartments/houses. Concerning buildings, some missional leaders believe that "New missional communities need to be established in places where unchurched people are comfortable gathering."[127] The missional church may emphasize community so much that basic Christian doctrines may be neglected, and teaching/preaching are put on the back-burner. Missional churches seek to incarnate the love of Christ in their community and neighborhood by helping people, feeding the hungry, serving others and one on one discipleship ministries. In their search for community and mission, some of these churches tend to criticize more traditional churches who do not specialize in these areas of ministry. Proponents of the missional model often criticize the traditional church with statements like, "Some popular missional church literature portrays the institutional church as a stale and mostly unattractive entity focused on maintaining its programs and buildings and increasingly unable to reach a secular society."[128] The missional church sees the institutionalized church as a place of hierarchy, buildings to maintain, structures to administrate with little flexibility to practically meet the needs of the churches' community neighbors and those in need.

---

[127] Effa, 373.
[128] Effa, 373.

The missional church proponents seek to recreate what they consider the ideal way to transform the community of which they are a part. They see the church attacking needs with great eagerness and helping family, friends, neighbors and the lost in general by meeting practical needs and sacrificing for the sake of others. Many inside the missional incarnation camp see the flexibility of small, informal groups more easily meeting these needs than an organized congregation. Speaking of the missional incarnation Church, Reggie McNeal in his 2011 work, *Missional Communities* says [of the Church], "It is best able to mirror the early days of the Jesus movement 'with particular attention to living lives of sacrifice and service to one another and to one's neighbor and not a set of religious activities.'"[129]

In *The Church as Movement: Starting and Sustaining Missional-Incarnational Communities* by J.R. Woodard and Dan White Jr. the emphasis on mission is so prevalent that the authors tend to neglect some doctrines and overemphasize and amplify other doctrines. In their book, these authors teach that everyone is to serve in one of the roles mentioned in Ephesians 4:13 of apostle, prophet, evangelist, pastor, or teacher. This teaching does much for the cause of empowering everyone equally, de-emphasizing the role of professional clergy, and moving towards plural church leadership. While some of those ideas may not be inherently bad, "It's best to see these offices as pertaining specifically to the leaders of the church who are then expected 'to equip the saints for the work of the ministry.'"[130] Much more alarming, Woodard and White also spend very little time explaining the death and resurrection of Jesus. It is noted that this is to be a

---

[129] McNeal, Reggie, "*Missional Communities: the Rise of the Post-Congregational Church*", 2011. San Francisco, California: Jossey-Bass.
[130] Gaines, Grant, "The Church as Movement: Starting and Sustaining Missional-Incarnartional Communities", Book Review, Themelios, 42 no 1 Apr 2017, p. 233. Harold Hunter Theological Library, Ebscohost, Accessed March 28, 2018.

disciple-making manual "with an entire section devoted to 'Sharing a Holistic Gospel.'"[131] It is curious as to why such a book would not devote more time to the death and resurrection of our Savior.

While no church model is perfect, including the Missional-Incarnational approach, it is worth noting that something has to be done to reverse the trend in the Churches diminishing impact across America. Even an author, Allan Effa, who is often critical of the missional movement, is quoted stating the realization that, "As the church in the West becomes increasingly marginalized and shrinks in numbers and influence, we are grappling with the daunting task of winning back a largely post-Christian society."[132] As this project is being written, Lifeway Christian Stores has just announced the closure of all of its American stores by the end of 2019. This leaves America with no national chain of Bible book stores. One is left to wonder how much of the demise of Lifeway has to do with the increasing digital revolution (Kindle, Nook, etc.), but also how much of the stores' closings have to do with less of a demand for American Christian resources in general?

8.2 Arguments Against the Missional Incarnational/ Emergent Church Approach

While Missional Communities have their share of valid criticism for the existing church, there is equally a fair amount of strong arguments for the continued effectiveness for the existing traditional Church and against Emergent/Missional praxis. Four of these points can be made when speaking of Church membership, organized church services, church buildings and the need for institutionalized movements.

---

[131] Gaines, 233.
[132] Effa, 374.

8.3 Church Membership is Not Irrelevant Today

Some missional communities downplay or speak against any type of official church membership. While a lively debate can be had concerning the lack of Biblical teaching on the matter and the process of how people become members, "check that box" and never return to the fellowship, membership does certainly have a place in the Kingdom. When you consider the concept of not having membership, and to the extreme, teaching against church membership - by default, you are actually teaching against having churches. Missional proponents of meeting casually in bars, barns and restaurants, teach that "By opting out of church membership they seek an alternative to a failed system, making way for the rise of the post congregational church [and] essentially this is a recipe for churchless Christianity."[133] When we do away with a formal membership process, that has in some way indoctrinated potential members and called them to abide by certain standards, then by default, we do away with the entire concept of a congregation. Membership provides belonging, purpose and official authorization to do the work of God.

I remember years ago when a teenager in my youth group was involved in what was called the "Goth," death or Marilyn Manson music culture at the time. He wanted nothing to do with God, and his mother forced him to come to church. One day, while he looked at me with a look like he wanted to kill me, I slipped him a note during church service. The note simply said, "Jesus loves you, I love you, and your mother loves you." Eventually, he had a radical conversion. He led many students at his school to Jesus, where his turnaround was very evident to all. One day he had been associated with a group known for defacing a Bible, and then a few months later, he was preaching in the cafeteria during lunch. As time went by, he was

---

[133] Effa, 377.

baptized in water. A few months passed, and he eventually, officially joined the church during a Sunday morning service. I will never forget visiting his house a few months later. While looking in his bedroom, I noticed something prominently displayed on his wall in a frame - his certificate of church membership. This piece of paper was not much more than a fifty-cent certificate purchased from the Bible book store and filled in by the pastor. This paper represented: identity, purpose, belonging, family and so much more. This official church membership is and was a reminder that the Church is the Body of Christ, and when one joins the Body, they become an important piece of that Body that is required in order that the entire Body function properly under the Lordship of Jesus. Membership in the Body asks something of its members, and it also comes with the benefits of fellowship, accountability, care, and significance. If we choose to no longer hold anyone to any standards of membership and accountability, it is difficult to rally the army of believers we call the church to corporately pool funds to make significant differences in disaster relief situations, plant new churches or send foreign and domestic missionaries. If the Church does not help someone find their identity in Christ, then often, gangs, cults, the wrong crowd, sports teams, civic organizations, and a myriad of other possibilities will fill this void. Membership means that the Church is something we take seriously because it is Christ's institution on earth.

8.4 Church Services Still Serve a Unique Purpose in Society

Another frequent criticism missional incarnational and emergent churches often level against the institutionalized church is that church services have little relevance to a modern citizen. In contrast, people simply want "relationship," and therefore the better route is to talk and eat together mainly with little thought for teaching doctrine. Once again, it may be true that the institutionalized church does not place enough emphasis on fellowship. Perhaps traditional churches (especially those that do not offer small groups or Sunday School classes) are lacking in offering opportunities for church members to meaningfully connect with one another. While community connection in the context of fellowship is very important, it is not mutually exclusive from organized church services. Whether the church service is an "attractional" larger, modern setting with theatrical lighting, contemporary sounding music and possibly even a smoke machine, or if it is the stellar opposite with a traditional setting, pastors wearing robes, high liturgy of creeds, congregational scripture readings and response with Holy communion, the weekly corporate church service has very distinct and unique purposes that are not (and mostly cannot be) fulfilled by a fellowship only model of church.

The weekly or more than weekly worship service has historically and continues to hold a place of great importance for the local fellowship of believers. This gathering is not a Parent Teachers Association Meeting; it is not the newest self-help meeting or the latest TED talk, it is not a classroom or even a group meeting of the local Alcoholics Anonymous - while all of these events may be good, they are completely different from a church service. The church service has elements that have NOTHING to do with fellowshipping or even serving your fellow man. In the church service,

> "Christian faith is nurtured and sustained by participation in a community that confesses its sins, is assured of God's forgiveness, listens to the Word, has its kingdom imagination sharpened through prayers of intercession for our broken world, and then is sent out, week after week, to be agents of transformation in the pathways of life. Attempting to live a churchless Christianity cuts one off from disciplines and patterns

that are very difficult to cultivate on one's own and contributes little or nothing toward the renewal of the church. Sipping cups of coffee...while building friendships with unchurched people is a wonderful expression of incarnational mission, but how long can such mission be faithfully expressed without the regular rhythms of gathering and sending?"[134]

The weekly church service is so unique that it offers something that cannot be duplicated even by internet video feeds or in coffee shops with just a few people. The church service is a place where God Himself is worshipped, sins are pointed out, AND forgiveness is offered, the Word is celebrated corporately, and we are commissioned to do the work of the Lord in the world for another week. The Ekklesia, or the called-out ones, are gatherers who come together to celebrate Jesus' life, death, and resurrection. This unique organization, meeting, and place in the world cannot be imitated or replaced by any other gathering. The power it brings to the Church community and the world that they serve and gather in is immeasurable.

8.5 Religious Church Buildings Can Set the Tone for Worship

Starting with the seeker-sensitive movement of the church, first popularized in the 1970s and 1980s by Willow Creek Community Church and Pastor Bill Hybels, many churches began to downplay their religiosity when building their meeting places. While Hybles was disgraced in a scandal in 2018 involving sexual misconduct[135], Hybels' impact (for better or for worse) on 25,000 weekly attendees

---

[134] Effa, 378.
[135] No Author given, "Following Up", Christian Century. 5/9/2018, Vol. 135 Issue 10, p18-18 Harold Hunter Theological Library, Ebscohost, Accessed April 12, 2018.

and millions of others who copied his church approach worldwide has greatly influenced Evangelical Christianity. Hybels was sure not to include crosses into the plans when he built the initial campus of Willow Creek Church, which eventually reached many thousands of people weekly in the Chicago area. The thinking was that the more unneeded roadblocks to the Church from unchurched people that we could remove - the better. This approach spilled over into the entire worship service and culture of Willow Creek. Services sometimes had popular, secular music, dramas to introduce the message and always considered not offending those in the pews. Interestingly, after several decades of this type of ministry, Willow Creek held the "Reveal" Study. The "Reveal" Study surveyed their church members and members of several other seeker-sensitive churches. The study revealed that their approach was failing miserably at truly discipling people who were very committed to the Lord. The church was reaching unchurched people and the new believers relatively well, but little growth was happening after the initial conversion and new believers experience. In the report, those identifying as "Close to Christ" or "Christ-Centered" (their two highest levels of commitment) expressed that they were "spiritually stalled" or "dissatisfied" with the role of the church in their spiritual growth and "63% were contemplating leaving the church".[136] Willow Creek basically reported that doing everything in an "un-churchy manner" did not produce deeply committed followers of Christ.

While it may be manifested differently, the seeker-sensitive approach when it comes to buildings has a lot in common with the missional incarnational approach. Seeker sensitive churches often build buildings that have no "trappings of religion" like crosses, religious art, or symbols. The Missional Incarnational Camp, possibly for the

---

[136] Branaugh, Mark. "Willow Creek's 'huge shift': influential megachurch moves away from seeker-sensitive services." *Christianity Today*, 52, no 6, Jun 2008, p 13.

sake of not spending money on it, do not place much or any value on religious buildings, preferring to use instead "neutral" or other meeting places that are not religious. Like church services which are valuable in their own way, religious church buildings are certainly not required for Christian worship, but they can serve an important role in worship. Environments often speak of the purposes for meetings. "Humans are context-sensitive communicators; the aesthetics and symbols that surround us convey an important part of a given message."[137] When traveling the United States, in a new town, you may see a barbershop display the immediately recognizable barber pole or place a graphic of it on their advertisement. The barber may also have a logo that displays a pair of scissors. Likewise, a dentist's office may have a picture or some representation of teeth in some fashion in their advertisements and displayed inside their office. It would be odd to us, if barbers were ashamed of the symbols of hair cutting or if dentists were ashamed of teeth. The Missional Incarnational communities and seeker-sensitive churches teach that we should minimize these religious symbols, and some especially push the minimization or removal of cross symbols. While most Christians understand that the symbol of a cross is just that, a symbol and Christ did not actually die on that religious symbol displayed in your church auditorium, the symbol itself may serve a tangible benefit of reminding people of what Jesus did on the actual cross of Calvary. While there is nothing wrong with meeting in a coffee house, hotel conference room, or movie theater, these places may not necessarily help the local church reach more people; they may also cause us to lose a little something that stained glass scenes portraying parables and miracles give us. When it comes to high steeple church buildings with their stained glass windows, communion tables, and praise and scripture banners, "Are these mere 'churchy' encumbrances that satiate the aesthetic

---

[137] Effa, 378.

thirst of the traditionalists while obscuring the true message of the radical Jesus, or are they anchors that ground our faith in something more substantial than a passing trend or fad?"[138]

8.6 Denominations and Movements Must Institutionalize if They are to Last

A final difficulty of the missional incarnational approach is the reluctancy to institutionalize as a local church. It is very easy to find fault with the "institutionalized" church-bishops, bureaucracies, scandals, politics; the list goes on and on and on. The word institution is defined as: *"a) an act of instituting : ESTABLISHMENT, a significant practice, relationship, or organization in a society or culture; also : something or someone firmly associated with a place or thing; b) an established organization or corporation (such as a bank or university) especially of a public character; c) a facility or establishment in which people (such as the sick or needy) live and receive care typically in a confined setting and often without individual consent."*[139] The word institution is not very appealing, and the definition has even less cool, hip and relevant words. "Firmly," "established," and "confined"- all words in the definition put off a crusty feel and push people away. These types of words are the exact reason why those in the missional/incarnational/emergent communities want to have nothing to do with the Church. Interestingly enough, it is this very institutional quality that is required at the exact same time to create a long-term organization that will outlast a founder or one group of contemporaries when they die. In a 2013, Christianity Today article, Andy Crouch noted that "Movements that fail to institutionalize are like seeds that spring up

---

[138] Effa, 379.

[139] *Merriam Webster s.v.* "institution," accessed April 12, 2019, https://www.merriam-webster.com/dictionary/institution.

quickly, but fail to become rooted."[140] Institutions maintain and carry on the DNA of an organization and movement once the initial founders are gone. Many have noted that "Human beings are, by necessity, dependent upon structures."[141] Entrepreneurial types of leaders, often are used by God to establish ministries and systems. These type of ministers are sought out to establish churches. When that leader dies, retires, or moves on for whatever reason, often the success or failure of the church after them will have much to do with how strongly the systems and (institutionalized) ministries were put into place. The new leaders, who are often not very entrepreneurial-minded (but may be harder workers and even more gifted in many ways), will simply carry on whatever was in place. This type of institutionalizing of the Church gives the new leaders a pattern and structure to follow, and if they were not in place, there would be no place for the new leader or church members to serve.

An institution's structures give automatic instructions on what to do and how to do it. These institutional structures have developed into networks of churches, denominational headquarters and regional offices, colleges and universities, missions systems, and ministerial credentialing bodies. While anything is possible, and all the more with God, it is unlikely that today's churches that meet in coffee houses or pubs will continue to flourish as an institution once the first generation of leaders are gone. If a "pastor" becomes absent by death, moral dis-qualification or the like, it will be needful to replace them with another leader. Generation one of the group may have a relationship with someone who is able to step in. If there is no network in place, the ministry may cease to exist. If there is a network in place (no matter how "un-institutional" it is), it will need to morph

---

[140] Crouch, Andy, "Planting deep roots: when you get serious about cultural change, you get serious about institutions" *Christianity Today*, 57, no 5, Jun 2013, p 61.
[141] Effa, 378.

into a more formal "institution" if it is to serve more than one church for any length of time. While with the Apostle Paul in the New Testament, we may not see a "professional" group of pastors, bishops, and leaders, we see the organization being put in place for elders, deacons, apostles, prophets, evangelists, pastors and teachers. These Body of Christ functions went on to form the first Church hierarchy and bureaucracy that would initially evolve into the many branches of the worldwide, institutionalized Church we see today. If there had not been the written Word (a very institutionalized thing to create) and the clear instructions of how to operate many facets of the church including leader qualifications and responsibilities, the Church, as we know it today, may not have existed some twenty centuries later. Speaking of those who believe that the institutional church is an institution that does not listen well to the Spirit, Effa says,"Restorationists tend to look at the dark side of Christian history while failing to acknowledge the work of the Holy Spirit in the councils hierarchies, theological developments, architecture, symbols, and liturgies that have sustained the life and mission of the global church."[142]

Allan Effa sums it up by saying, "If the church is really so hopelessly broken, how has it produced countless saintly examples whose lives mirror the radical love and ministry of Jesus?"[143] The American church is certainly at a crossroads, which may determine its long term health and even survival. Missional/Incarnational leaders, attractional groups like ARC, house church leaders, satellite campus leaders, and traditional pastors all have their own idea of what the American Church of the future should look like. Only God knows what the Church will and should look like, how prevalent it will be or not be and when Jesus will return. Until then, we can learn from

---

[142] Effa, 377.
[143] Effa, 376.

all types of churches and start new ones and apply what the Spirit leads us to do using a combination of varying strategies, but we must continue to start churches of every kind.

CHAPTER 9

URBAN CHURCH PLANTING

9.1 Urban Church planting and specifically in New York City

Urban church planting is a different animal than suburban or rural planting. While suburban and rural church plants have their own challenges, the urban church planter will face challenges that are not just different because of possibly higher crime and population density, but the urban church plant in a megacity such as New York will have to contend with real estate pricing challenges. Global cities such as New York have special considerations that drastically impact the formation, growth, and health of high-density urban congregations. This section will discuss: a model for urban church planting from Barquisimeto, Venezuela (a city with a metro of more than one million people), the ethnic/racial reality of mega, "melting pot" city church planting and particular challenges connected to premium city real estate prices in New York City.

9.2 A Model for Urban Church Planting: Barquisimeto, Venezuela

James Tino and Paul Brink wrote an extended article in *Missio Apostolica* called, "A Model for Urban Church Planting, the First Phase: From Preliminary Investigation to First Worship Service". In 1999, they laid out a plan that successfully planted a church in Barquisimeto, Venezuela with 25 people that grew to more than 80 in four years' time with all new converts. The city was characterized by "strong resistance" to the Gospel (as many large cities are), and only 3% of the population were practicing Christians.[144] While some of the articles show age, it is a good resource that lays a foundation for a traditional style church plant in a city environment.

Tino and Brink lay out the plan in Four Stages: Stage I Preliminary Investigation, Stage II Moving into the City, Stage III Beginning the Work, and Stage IV Developing a Worshipping Community. Before starting, the pair gives this advice: "1) pray regularly 2) Be creative, open-minded, and flexible 3) If you choose to follow this guide do things in order! 4) Don't assume that something written here does not apply to your situation until you have first tried it out!"[145]

In Stage I: Preliminary Investigation - you should seek to discover where to live, population targets, and the amount of money needed to get started. The pair suggest 15 days to one month for on-site evaluation and investigation. They recommend identifying: city geography and structure, population breakdown, socio-economic distribution, real estate costs and religious life.[146]

---

[144] Tino, James and Brink, Paul "A Model for Urban Church Planting, the First Phase: From Preliminary Investigation to First Worship Service", *Missio Apostolica*, 7 Mar 1999, p 40.

[145] Tino and Brink, 40.

[146] Tino and Brink, 41.

In Stage II: Moving into the City, the timeframe suggested is four months. During Stage II, it is recommended to write a mission statement, secure missionary (or church planter) housing and secure a ministry center (offices that can accommodate 20 or 30 people meeting in them for Bible studies and renting a separate space for worship services later as the ministry grows). It is recommended that security/safety, ease of public transportation to the ministry center and distance from the ministry housing be strongly considered in this process. The creators of this model of urban ministry discourage starting the work in the home of the missionary couple as a "limiting" strategy that can also "compromise the missionary couple."[147]

Stage III: Beginning the Work calls for a 12-month timeframe to complete. In this stage, it is recommended to: 1) NOT begin worship services but hold simple Bible studies only because worship services consume more than 20 hours a week in preparation time 2) hire secretary/clerical worker to make calls; be a receptionist, keep up with people. The mission in Venezuela also hired a two-day-a-week errand boy. 3) Develop contacts by holding activities to attract people, attempt to get people to interact with each other at these events, gather their contact information. Suggestions include English as a Second Language Classes, Family Movie Nights, and Friendship Sunday Worship days. During this stage it is recommended to: NOT fill time with anything other than evangelistic attempts, do not only have the missionary as the only point of contact between new contacts, do not only have home events as it will be hard to get people to come to anything that is not at a home if this is all you have done up until this point, do not dedicate large amounts of time to the 'socially marginalized' as you are trying to develop a church by reaching the entire

---

[147] Tino and Brink, 42.

community, and do not set bad precedents like bringing everyone to church in your car.[148]

Stage IV of the plan is "Developing a Worshipping Community." Tino and Brink recommend developing a simple, weekly Bible study that will correlate to the times that will eventually become a worship service. In the study, it is recommended to not yet have music and to not teach in a systematic way where you needed to be at the last session to build upon and understand what is happening at the next teaching session. It is recommended to have a mid-week study for those who have accepted Christ as Savior. It is recommended again to NOT start regular worship services too soon. Holding full-blown worship services require massive amounts of time that could better be used for evangelism during this phase.

Other recommendations include: pray for musicians, widely publicize the first worship service because you only have a "first service" once, get as many people involved as possible working in areas like ushering, greeting, Sunday School, set up/tear down, opening/closing the building and visitation. Using this model, within a year and a half, the church should be celebrating a first anniversary and moving toward self-sufficiency.[149]

9.3 Global and Urban City Church Planting Considerations: language/ethnicity and real estate challenges

Cities of approximately one million or more metro population usually have many things in common. Megacities of about 10 million often have extreme similarities, and these unique characteristics of large and mega cities can even be observed in many larger cities of 350,000 to half a million or so. These cities are often crowded with

---

[148] Tino and Brink, 43-44.
[149] Tino and Brink, 45-46.

people from around the globe, and when these immigrants come, they often bring with them their own religious traditions. This religious melting pot creates a lessened percent of Christian Churches in the religious marketplace as much of the religious market place is now taken up by Buddhist temples, Mosques, and Hindu places of worship.[150] Some of the distinctive features of these larger cities to be considered in a church planting paradigm include real estate price limitations, mass transit convenience, language/cultural and ethnic identity barriers.

In America, New York City is the greatest example of cultural diversity, an ethnic "melting pot" center, and real estate limitations. The language barrier has no equal to New York, "While there is no precise count, some experts believe New York is home to as many as 800 languages — far more than the 176 spoken by students in the city's public schools."[151] New York is the most linguistically diverse city in the world, and the language barrier presents a significant obstacle in many, if not most, major cities in America and globally. In many large cities, areas become filled with similar ethnic and language groups, examples - "Chinatowns," "Koreatowns," or "Little Italys." Depictions of micro ethnic communities can be seen in 1980 fantasy films like "Gremlins" and "Big Trouble in Little China." These ethnic communities are very pronounced in megacities like New York. New York has the largest "Chinatown" on the east coast. Surprisingly, New York City's largest Chinatown is not in Manhattan where most tourists may be familiar with Canal Street Chinatown. Actually, New York's, and the east coast's largest "Chinatown" is downtown Flushing, New York. Flushing is a part of New York City which is an urban center

---

[150] Buntain, Ian B, "Church Planting in the Secular West: Learning from the European Experience", Themelios, 42, no 3, December 2017, p 591.
[151] Roberts, Sam, "Listening to (and Saving) the World's Languages", New York Times, April 29, 2010.

in the borough of Queens.[152] As of 2006, Flushing was more than 50% Asian. "Fifty-seven percent of these Asians were Chinese, while Koreans made up twenty-seven percent."[153]

Queens is itself known as an incredibly diverse area within New York City. On the 2000 census form, residents of Queens listed that they spoke 138 different languages.[154] While these languages make a city very interesting to visit, they can be large barriers to reaching a people group. In Flushing, Queens of New York for example, Chinese and Korean churches must negotiate for similar spaces to plant houses of worship, and there can be what the author of one article makes sound like a bit of a religious turf war between competing Christian groups. In Flushing, for example, when you consider all faiths (Christian churches, Buddhist temples, Hindu temples, Mosques, and Sikh Temples), "Two hundred different houses of worship are densely populated in a residential neighborhood and commercial district [in] about two-point-five square miles."[155] Flushing initially became overcrowded by new immigrants when "Cheap real estate prices for available spaces were the main attraction for many Asian immigrants."[156]

Today, Flushing real estate is in no way inexpensive and in some cases can be somewhat similar to real estate pricing in parts of Manhattan, just a few miles away. Homogeneous foreign language groups, who once had many options of where to inexpensively plant a new church in New York City, now have serious issues finding a place. As more and more immigrants migrate to the states, as well as second and third generation people of these groups are born as Americans

---

[152] Pae, Keun-joo Christine, "Negotiated or Negotiating Spaces: Korean Churches in Flushing, Queens of New York City", *Cross Currents*, 58, no 3, Fall 2008, p 456.
[153] Pae, 459.
[154] Roberts, Sam.
[155] Pae, 458.
[156] Pae, 459.

in New York, real estate options are more limited. The explosion of one of these groups and their churches can be seen in a dramatic way in Flushing. The Korean Council of Churches in Greater New York says that the first Korean Church in Flushing was founded in 1969. As of 2003, this group officially registered 200 Korean churches in Flushing, but believed there may be 500 Korean churches in Flushing if one counts "non-council member churches and non-denominational, small house churches."[157] This fact is staggering, but one must consider its two-fold consequences. On the positive side, Korean Christianity in Flushing has grown tremendously. Therefore, we see it is possible for anything to happen in New York City with the Lord's help. Just as the Korean Churches have multiplied in Flushing, Queens over just a few decades, this can happen with any Church group. On the negative side, as the Korean, Chinese and Pakistani populations have also increased remarkably in Flushing, so has the scarcity of potential locations to establish houses of worship and to increase the size of the existing church locations. Over the course of the last few decades, Korean Churches and Koreans in general, have reported that Koreans have been forced out of downtown Flushing.

> *"As Chinatown has expanded, the building owners, who rented their spaces to Koreans, either sold their properties to Chinese or rented spaces to them because the Chinese offered better prices."[158] "Reverend J. Kim, whose church facilities are located a couple of blocks away from downtown [Flushing]…remembered that Main Street was once filled with Korean stores…Now his facilities are located between an exclusively Chinese area and the edge of Koreatown. He believes that it was*

---

[157] Pae, 460.
[158] Pae, 461.

God's grace for his church to buy the building twenty years ago, otherwise, his church would not be able to own the building in Flushing."[159]

Just as existing congregations have difficulty securing church spaces to launch a new work, much could also be said for the difficulties faced by densely urban churches who must deal with large zoning ordinances as well. Often large churches are maxed out in places like New York because of their inability to purchase or secure more rental space for expansion. Many zoning laws have mandated how many parking spots are required for church buildings, which are often next to impossible to meet in a megacity. In reaction to such laws, some churches have found loopholes by using folding chairs (which the number can be varied, instead of fixed pews) and creating valet parking services. Other churches are sharing facilities across denominational lines, such as the Q Catholic (Korean) Church in Flushing, which sometimes utilizes the Salvation Army Church (next door) for parking and playground facilities.[160] Zoning and parking are serious considerations in large cities, but churches will hopefully continue to find creative ways to work around these and other obstacles to the formation and numerical growth.

This is an example of how churches struggle in densely populated places to both find a place where the primary ethnic or language group can meet together (considering housing, availability of mass transportation) and at the same time be in a location where the group can afford to buy or lease a facility large enough to hold their worship services. In the same article, Pae notes that the Chinese had just moved into a grocery store space in Bayside, Queens, which is an area adjacent to Flushing. While the article's emphasis on this fact

---

[159] Pae, 461.
[160] Pae, 467.

was that the Chinese were taking even more ground that was once somewhat Korean space, it is also noted that the space the grocery store was going to occupy had been vacant for a while. The reason it had been vacant was that the rent for, "the Chinese grocery store had been abandoned for a while due to one million dollar(s) rent per year."[161] While most average-sized churches cannot imagine building a permanent building for a cost of $1 million. How many could consider renting a relatively small space for $1 million per year? The reality of these figures are from 2003-2008, much more eleven years later. While these considerations probably seem far-fetched for midsized, large and mega-church congregations in the U.S. South, it may be advantageous for these churches to hold onto what may seem like older buildings on the "wrong side of town" today. In time, as large towns develop into cities, and as cities develop into large cities…what may seem as less than desirable real estate today can easily be sought after in just the passing of one to two generations. In the American south, church growth experts have all types of formulas for how many parking spaces are required to grow a church to a specific size. In New York and many other global cities, if you have a parking lot of any kind at all, it is often considered a tremendous luxury and bonus.

The complications of pioneering works in densely populated cities are not confined only to real estate prices and language barriers. Cities that have large groups of immigrants that come from a variety of ethnic and cultural differences also tend to self-segregate into their own little areas. New York City claims to have citizens from at least 148 countries.[162] A recent report also brought to light that, "Over 37 percent of New York City residents were born in another country …the highest percentage in over 100 years. A record-high 3.07 million foreign-born immigrants live in New York City, more

---

[161] Pae, 461.
[162] Gregor, Allison, "How to Fill a Melting Pot", New York Times, June 11, 2013.

than any other city in the world."¹⁶³ As the article that has been cited much from Keun-joo Christine Pae seems to bring to light at least some level of tension between the Koreans and the Chinese of Flushing, varying ethnic groups also tend to see other differences, not related to the country of origin or language. Pae says of Koreans, "Spiritual enthusiasm and dedication to the church are two factors to differentiate Korean Christians from other religious (groups) as well as from non-Korean Christians."¹⁶⁴ While there may be some truth to this statement, it is difficult to believe that all Korean Christians are more spiritually enthusiastic and dedicated to the Church than all Chinese Christians or as the last part of the quote claims than "from (*all*) non-Korean Christians." This type of stereotyping of their own group is possibly a part of the reason why groups seem to self-segregate. While there are certainly many Korean Christians with "outward-church" attendance and "out-ward spiritual fervor", most Anglo Christians, and many people in all groups of Christianity and ethnicities also display extremely high levels of spiritual enthusiasm and church attendance.

Just as Pae sees her ethnic group as unique and some might argue spiritually superior in some ways (worship attendance and fervor), other groups, often do the very same thing. Martin Luther King, Jr. made the observation over half a century ago that, "We must face the sad fact that at eleven o'clock on Sunday morning when we stand to sing 'In Christ, there is no East or West,' we stand in the most segregated hour of America."¹⁶⁵ As long as Christians do not hate or oppose

---

[163] No author given, "More Foreign-Born Immigrants Live in NYC Than There Are People In Chicago," Huffpost (blog), 12/1913, updated Dec. 6, 2017. as accessed April 15, 2019. https://www.huffpost.com/entry/new-york-city-immigrants_n_4475197

[164] Pae, 465.

[165] Biney, Moses O., "Building Bridges in New York City: Starting With Churches", *The Living Pulpit (Online)*, 24, no 1, Spring 2015, p. 14-16. as accessed November 18, 2018. through the Ebscohost, Harold Hunter Theological Library.

each other due to race or ethnic cultural expression, possibly, separate communities can be understood and may not be an indication of prejudicial bias or racism; however, we are reminded in scripture that in heaven, every tribe, nation, and race will be represented *(see Revelation 7:9)*, seen and accounted for. If we could learn to love and accept each other now, cross lines as Jesus tells us to do in the story of the Good Samaritan *(see Luke 10:25-37)*, we will be preparing for heaven now. While language is obviously the most understandable barrier to cohabitation of cultures in existing churches, even it can be addressed through the use of interpreters (even though people may easily complain of the inconvenience of interpretation in church services). May the Lord help us all, love each other, and more than tolerate but embrace different cultures, people, races, and divisions which may un-biblically feel someway or anyway, superior to one another. It is God's intention that every person and tribe on the planet come to the saving knowledge of Jesus Christ through the Holy Spirit. This will not be accomplished until we selflessly love people who are different than us, at least a little different than us, in small, insignificant ways on the outside.

CHAPTER 10

Breaking Church Growth Attendance Barriers for the Small Church

Many books and articles have been written on breaking attendance barriers. Like most of this book, I do not claim originality, but this book will try to bring four ideas to light on the subject. It has been my experience with most church growth seminars and books that when discussing breaking barriers, almost always 200 or 500 are keyed in on. Interestingly, many times, the pastors who are sent to these trainings by denominations or who pay to go to them themselves, are pastoring less than 100 people on a given Sunday. Little is said to the pastor who faithfully pastors 30 or 40 people year after year. Many of these pastors started those churches themselves and should be greatly commended for pastoring 40 people. Anyone who pastors 40 people actually, normally truly shepherds about 120 people, they just never show up all at the same time, and many of these pastors are also the primary caregiver to their members' family, extended family, and friends. This is the reason that so many small churches who do very little in the way of administration and outreach still consistently have three times as many people in attendance for Easter services, Christmas plays, and Homecoming or other special events. It is this pastor who is called upon to visit third cousins in the hospital, to do the funeral for the neighbor of the church member who never attends church regularly and it is this pastor who will be asked to perform marriage counseling for the board member's thirty-year-old son even though that same child quit attending church when they graduated high school. On "big days" (Holidays, special events, kids programs, etc.), it is often revealed who the church truly "ministers to" and who say they attend the church even though they may not come regularly more than 2-4 times a year. The pastors of "40" to "50" person churches often assist 120-150 people in their spiritual walk just as the pastor of a "2,000" person church actually "ministers to" 6,000 people or more. For this reason, it is imperative that the pastor of a church of 30 or 40 people in attendance quit doing all that they are doing - because they are doing more than they realize.

The first idea concerning Breaking Church Growth Barriers -

10.1- Pastor, Quit being the primary or only caregiver

In their classic book "How to Break Growth Barriers: Revise your role, release your people and capture overlooked opportunities for your church" by Carl F. George and Warren Bird, the authors continually beat home one central idea. The idea is that if the pastor is the "primary caregiver," they will almost never reach 200 people or anywhere near it.[166] In other words, if the pastor has to run to the hospital, not just for the heart attacks and stage three cancer diagnosis, but especially if they must go to the hospital for a broken finger

---

[166] Carl F. George, and Warren Bird. *How to Break Growth Barriers*. (Grand Rapids, MI: Baker Books, 1993, updated 2017), 29.

during a skateboarding accident and to accompany someone for a routine test, there it will be very difficult to build a church of any size.

The mentality of many small churches is that the pastor is "hired" to do the ministry, and the church leadership will simply pay them and, if needed, tell them what to do. This is not the mentality of the mid-size, large, or megachurch. In the larger church (usually - not always), a team of people are in place to minister to needs, and the pastor is a part of this and the leader of this. However, more of the pastor's time will be spent teaching others to minister and care for people than will be spent doing this himself. The truth is that many pastors and churches are very co-dependent on each other. It does make the pastor feel good and important to be liked and needed at the hospital. It is a warm fuzzy that will often endear the person who is sick to the pastor. If this is needed psychologically for the pastor though, it will inevitably 1) stop the growth of the church or 2) kill or nearly kill the pastor in the process.

Most people can only maintain about 50 vitally important relationships. If you have a family, hopefully, those relationships will be first. So if you have a family of five, you are already down to 45. Some "super" pastors, can stretch that dynamic to up to 200 people. This is very difficult and taxing at best, but if you can make this happen (and some glutton for punishment pastors have even stretched it to 400 -700 people) you will almost always burn out. If you do not burn out emotionally and spiritually, most of these pastors (which I have been one of them) will have a heart attack, drop dead, or experience other major health issues that force them out of the ministry altogether.

When I was 30, I was speaking to a class of new members at a 2 pm afternoon session. Earlier that day, I had preached a 9 am service (that I also played the drums at), taught a 10 am Sunday School class, and again played the drums and preached at 11:15 am. While I was speaking at the New Members Class, everything went black and I collapsed. Upon getting to the hospital it was discovered that an ulcer had eaten into the wall of my colon as a result of me taking up to (believe it or not) 20-40 B.C. Powders, Stan Back Headache Powder or Goody's Extra Strength Headache Powders to ward off the relentless headaches that I dealt with almost daily. I had got to the point that for the previous seven years, I was taking them almost every day. Often, I would take 3-4 powders at a time with nothing to drink (this is a special developed talent that you would have to have ever tasted these aspirin powders to appreciate). The doctors informed me that he thought I was probably a few hours away from death and kept me in the hospital for more several days. Fortunately, for me, I learned a lesson, took the physician's advice, and with the Lord's help - never took aspirin again in my life and only ate salads for 90% of the time over the next year to give my body the opportunity to heal.

I was a little insane, self-centered, and prideful enough to think that I was the only person that could perform all those tasks. At that time, like many pastors, I had serious problems with thinking I was more important than I was. I'm sure I may still think I am more important than I am from time to time, but most of the time, I am more grounded in reality as the hair has become less abundant, the back sometimes has caused issues, and the energy level of the mid-forties is greatly different than that of the 26-year-old, know it all, new church planter. The truth is, many other people could have played the drums or taught Sunday School and the New Members Class. It was not just Sundays, I lived a lot of my life like that as if I was the savior of the church who needed to do about 80% of the work of the church. When we do this, it takes away from other people's God-given gifting that they are called to use in the church and put people's attention on us and off of the real Savior. Over the course of three days in the hospital (in a double room with a man dying of AIDS next to me), I had a lot of time to consider how I had been living and how I was not interested in dying at the age of 30.

Interestingly enough, at the time I was doing all of that, the church was only running a total of about 100-120 people most of the time (sometimes less than 100). Over the next few years, the church would grow to double the size, but my management style would change drastically as we instituted several training programs that raised up volunteer elders and deacons, lay congregational care ministers and paid pastors to minister to people. Many other pastors have stories that ended in death, health issues that removed them from ministry completely or emotional and spiritual problems that crowded out Jesus to the point that "ministry" became more important until they lost their relationship with Christ altogether and in the process many a church, marriage, family relationship and more went down in flames as well.

At the time, I was being hospitalized with a life-threatening, self-inflicted illness - I was not backslidden in the sense that I did not truly love Jesus and His church, but the time with Jesus was often rushed. When you have to fit in a prayer meeting or private and family devotions between "saving" the people of the church - there is a lot of pressure there. If you have 8 people to visit in the hospital, 6 phone calls to make about who missed church last week, meet with the secretary about how the money was on Sunday, a Wednesday night Bible study to prepare, 4 counseling sessions with church members who need marriage help, a funeral to prepare for on Thursday, two morning services and Sunday School to prepare for, for Sunday morning and do not forget Sunday night, 2 kids at home who need you at soccer practice and the third grade band recital, and a wife that just might want to occasionally see you - it is hard to find a couple hours for Jesus. I mean come on, look how important I am to all these folks! Surely the Lord understands. During these years, I managed to spend time with the Lord every day or almost every day, but it was often a rushed, hurried experience. There is something about a stress level that is a constant 8 or 9 on a scale of 1-10 that makes it difficult for the Word to permeate your Spirit in such a way that it changes your soul. It is difficult to hear what the Lord is saying when you are really thinking, *"Come on and just say it Holy Spirit! You know I do not have time for this waiting stuff!"* The pastor, who does it all, does not have proper time for God. The pastor who has proper time for God, putting Him first, it seems as if the Lord changes the rest of the pastor's time to make the important stuff fit into the schedule.

The "How to Break Growth Barriers" book, and most every other book and seminar on the subject all say basically the same thing, over and over and over - the pastor must not be the primary caregiver if they are going to be a part of a church of much size at all. The idea is for the pastor to become a pastor of pastors. This can be accomplished through many ways, including systems of elders and deacons (who actually minister to people - not just have a title so that they may perform business functions of the church), lay ministry empowerment where people are given responsibility for certain families in the church for their nurture and spiritual care and the number recommendation is commonly through small groups. These small groups may initially be Sunday School groups, but as the Sunday School classes are maxed out, then you hit a glass ceiling. This can be broken by adding two or sometimes in very large churches even three Sunday School hours, but there will always be a point at which there are no more rooms to fill. This is one of the reasons that small groups or house churches in people's house, not a centralized church location - is almost always more effective than Sunday School. Sunday School also places the cost of curriculum, utilities and group facilities upkeep on the central church, where in-home small groups or house churches, places the financial burden on the local group.

This arrangement allows the central church to flourish and have less chance for bottlenecking at certain facilities maximum usage. When utilizing members' homes, there will always be ample homes as the church grows because more homes will be available.

Truth is many very small churches like the pastor doing all the work. In some mean-spirited, vindictive churches (yes, they are out there), the church members almost like to torture the pastor with their demands, and the smaller the church, the more the demands. I will never forget when I was preaching in a church as a guest on a Sunday night one time when in this church of about 80 people on normal Sunday morning when a retired, but very able-bodied woman raised her hand with a verbal prayer request. The retired woman raised her hand to explain that a person who was barely connected to the church was sick. She explained how she was very close to the woman relationally. She then asked could the church pray for the woman. The pastor said yes, of course. Then before she sat down, she added that the pastor "needed to go visit her tomorrow," and the pastor said he would. It took everything in me to not grab the microphone and say, "What is holding you up from visiting this woman since she is so dear to you?" This was this churches' usual practice, and they quickly cycle through good pastors every year or so for many years.

The changing of the pastor to being a shepherd of shepherds and not the only or primary caregiver is the mega stumbling block for churches that desire to break the 150-ish barrier, but of course, there are other barriers below 200. Almost every barrier will be more easily broken if the pastor has the mindset that they should train others to minister well, but there are other very basic things that will hinder the church at 50, 100, or 150 or so as well…

The second idea concerning Breaking Church Growth Barriers

10.2- Pastor, Quit literally doing almost everything.

I started this book by saying it is dedicated to pastors who cut the grass, visit the hospitals, and prepare the bulletins, and more. This is true because many of these pastors are very dedicated and sincere in their efforts to grow the Kingdom of God through the local church that they are called to lead. These same pastors could often be much more effective if they allowed others to do the work of the ministry with them.

I know of one hardworking pastor who mowed his churches' grass every week for years on end. It was a matter of pride for him. The problem is that every time those church people saw that the grass was mowed very well, they had no reason to mow it themselves. The more a pastor does for the people, the less of a need for the people to do much of anything. People's natural tendency is to be lazy, and if the pastor helps them be lazy, most people will sit back, relax in their Lay-Z-Boys and cheer for the pastor as he mows the grass, cleans the bathrooms and does whatever else his heart is content to do. These types of tasks are often done at no cost to the church. The sacrificial spirit of the pastor is admirable, but may I suggest that if you are going to do something long term as the pastor that you would often pay others to do, that you go ahead and pay the pastor (with the churches' approval) for tasks such as cleaning the bathrooms or cutting the grass. The reason this is suggested is that at least the pastor will receive financial compensation for these tasks because the chances are that if the pastor is doing these types of tasks on a continual basis for more than say 6 months (for a good temporary reason possibly) the church is never, ever going to grow. The pastor has limited energy and time, and these types of things are not time in the Word or prayer - the two New Testament tasks that pastors are clearly called to spend their time doing. The most beneficial thing that the pastor can do for the church is to be in the Word and spending as much time as possible in prayer. Prayer often adds energy. The Word adds life and wisdom. Time with God enlightens, frees and changes us for the better. The more time the pastors spend in the presence of God, the more attractive and fruitful their preaching and teaching ministry will be. Time cleaning toilets or cutting grass (while it can be a sweet sacrifice performed unto the Lord) still takes away from our time with the Lord, depletes physical energy resources, hinders time that could be spent teaching others to do these very simple tasks that almost anyone could do and robs others of this opportunity for Kingdom service for those who are called with the gift of helps.

Probably some of the desire to do everything yourself comes from the idea that it must be done "well." This is a problem with people who cannot delegate. As a young minister, my pridefulness made me think that few people could do a lot of things as good as I could do them. If you think this about a lot of things 1) you are probably fooling yourself and 2) even if it is true in a number of areas, people do not have to be as good at something as you are, they only need to be able to do it to a satisfactory standard. Likewise, they do not have to be able to do it just like how you would do it; they just have to be able to do it. Some say that a person must only be able to do what you are doing at 80% the capacity that you could do it to let go of the task and some say as high as 90% or as low as 60%, but the point is that they will never get better at the task at hand until they are doing it themselves and you will never be free of it until someone else is doing it. The more you give away things to do, the more you empower people and the less you will have to do. Some people think that doing everything makes you important, but the reality is the more you give away, not the more you keep, the more important you become. It's true in money, and it's true in everything else.

The small church pastor also may want everything to be done well because they believe that everything is done better and with excellence in the large church and that the major difference in the large church and the small church is excellence. While there is some truth to the fact that larger churches generally or at least often do some things better than smaller churches, and while if your church is going to grow there will need to be some production excellence in the services and programs offered, I think that this is often over-blown in the mind of the small church pastor.

I personally know of a church of around 500 that is (or at least when it was growing 20 years ago) CONSUMED with excellence. No one was good enough to do almost anything. This did create some growth, but it was more of the pastor's overworking of himself and the staff that created much of the growth. On the other hand, when I went to work at a church of more than 5,000, I expected that everything would be so much better in every way. Some things certainly were - the buildings and facilities were much larger and nicer, the music was possibly slightly better, and the amount of staff was much larger. On the other hand, the amount of "excellence" out of volunteers was certainly no higher than the church of 500. The difference and what they were better at, was getting more people involved. The larger church had more people in choirs, singing, playing instruments, working in the nursery and kids church, tons of ushers and greeters, light people, sound people, computer people, intercessory prayer warriors, 50 elders, deacons, pastors of every kind, communion servers, small group leaders and most of all they had a highly paid pastoral staff position that was in charge of nothing but "Teams". The teams' person was a quiet, behind the scenes guy. He hardly ever spoke or was even seen in public, but he was probably the most important staff member in the entire church. As the youth pastor, I was hired to lead teams. I had 2 assistant paid youth pastors and a full-time youth secretary as well as more than 20 very dedicated youth-adult workers. The youth department was just a small version of all the teams that were in the entire church.

I discovered, much to my surprise, that sometimes people who were not SUPER qualified to do things in this church were allowed to do it anyway. Even though the pastor was a genius of a man, his standards were not so incredibly high that they could not be reached by mere mortals. In the church of 500, it was often not this way, but in the church of 5,000, if people were willing to do something and had a good attitude, there was a really good chance they were going to be allowed and encouraged to do it. The only thing that they were more excellent at was getting people involved.

Pastors of small churches often hold people back from doing things because they believe that their people are not as qualified to do something as possibly the folks at the church down the road, which is the size of a small city. In truth though, the old adage is true, God doesn't call the qualified, He qualifies the called. He is still more interested in ability than availability. This is not just a preaching cliché, but it is a motto that growing churches live by.

The third idea concerning Breaking Church Growth Barriers

10.3 Get People Involved in Doing Something (Anything that is Good and Productive).

A principle of church growth has to do with how many people will come watch a friend or family member do something. Possibly said first by Rev. Billy Graham, "For every person involved, three to four people will come to watch them do it." When it comes to gathering a gigantic crowd at a stadium event like Billy Graham's crusades or when it comes to gathering a group to fill a local church auditorium, this statement (or a variation of it) is generally true. In other words, if you have a choir, for each choir member, normally 1-5 people will come to listen to and watch them sing. If this was a very outspoken, extroverted, big personality choir member, they may be able to convince 5-10 people to come to the crusade or church service. Even the quietest, least influential person will still often be able to get at least one person to come with them if they are meaningfully involved in a church event. Because of this principle, it is a wonderful idea that the pastor gets as many people involved in as many ministries as possible. Not only does this help the person performing the ministry task find meaning and purpose in the Church and life in general, but it also pulls others in to possibly hear the Word of God and be changed eternally. Additionally, having more people involved increases overall church attendance and congregational morale. While this may be difficult for the pastor of the small church to come up with something for a lot of people to do every week, it is easier to plan for a limited time for special events such as Christmas programs, Easter events, Friend's Days, Fourth of July Celebrations and the like. If the church can have the building full for special events, they just might like it and decide to invite people more often. Growing churches understand this and do everything in their power to get as many people as involved as possible, as quickly as possible.

As an example, before understanding these principles as a youth pastor and later on as a senior pastor who led the youth on Wednesday evenings myself, I never had more than about 50 coming consistently to our youth group. Once I implemented these principles in our youth ministries (had many youth caregivers [small group leaders who pastored their own youth teams within the youth group] and built many youth ministries within the youth ministry [youth music, layers of youth pastors and assistant youth pastors, youth data administrators who kept up with youth, youth game people who planned games, etc.]) our youth group grew to more than 130-150 every week and sometimes had 200 teens for youth service. Interestingly, when I was trying to do most of everything myself as a youth pastor while working in churches from 500 to 5,000 with almost unlimited youth budgets and facilities, it was hard to get 150 teens. Later, when I was the senior pastor of a church of several hundred congregants, I had very little time for youth ministry. While pastoring the church, I knew it was impossible for me to give youth more than one day a week. This forced me to train leaders in my place. Within a few years, our church consistently ran about 140 teens weekly with nights close to 200 even though we had limited facilities, budgets and I had very little time to commit to the youth ministry. When you determine that others will have to get the job done or it will not get done, then it will probably get done if you have trained and then trusted others with the ministry.

The fourth idea concerning Breaking Church Growth Barriers

10.4 If you lean to being a perfectionist (or at least excellence) in pastoring and ministry - then quit being so concerned with quality and get more concerned with quantity.

Before you read any further, remember that I first said, "If you lean to being a perfectionist." I am a recovering perfectionist. Perfect people are very difficult to get along with because you never can meet their standards, but the truth is that often, the perfectionists cannot meet their own standards, and that is why so many perfectionists are difficult to be around. If you are always demanding that you and everything around you are perfect, then you will never be happy with much of anything in this life. Having said that striving for excellence in ministry is an entirely different thing. Excellence is not always perfect, but it is putting your best foot forward and presenting a church service that is representative of the worthy God that we serve. Some churches do not strive for perfection (which is good), but they equally do not strive for excellence in ministry (which is bad). If you are not striving for excellence in all that is done on your church ministry, then just stop reading right here, ignore the last advice in this book. Having set forth the disclaimer that all churches should strive for excellence, then here comes the rest of the point - quit being so concerned with quality and more concerned with quantity.

Problem: Lack of Church Member Involvement - often, the smaller a church is, the less people are involved. In a group of 20 people, it is very common for the pastor to be in charge of everything, lead all the ministries and manage all the business of the church. Many times pastors will say that they cannot find "qualified" people to fulfill the various roles in the church, so they are "forced to do it all themselves." In larger churches, often a staff member or many staff members are employed full-time to do nothing except for getting people involved (which throws back to point 3).

Solution: Get People Involved-

I remember the first time that I worked in a church of more than 300 people when I was 21 years old. I was amazed that some of the people that were heavily involved had SERIOUS flaws. From the outside looking in, this church seemed to only use people that "had it together." The church was primarily made up of white-collar professionals. While I am sure many of these talented and bright individuals did actually pretty much "have it together" in the world's eyes, I was surprised behind the scenes at how many were attending counseling for a variety of serious problems. I was not judgmental of them - as a young man, I was insecure that I was not "good enough" to work at a "prestigious" church like this. I soon discovered the reality was that no matter how we dress or talk, no matter what letters or professional designations came before or after our names and titles, we are all people CONTINUALLY in need of a Savior. The case is not that before we accepted Christ as Savior that we needed a Savior then, but still today and every day, we daily depend on Christ through the power and person of the Holy Spirit to keep us and mold us more into His image. I realized quickly that the church was not a museum of saints but a hospital for sinners who had been called saints by the redemptive work of Calvary. In short order, I realized that for a church to grow, people had to be involved. In my time at this church, it grew from 280 to 600 in weekly attendance and had big days several times a year with more than 1,000 attendees. During my time at this church, the people being involved in ministry did not become perfect, but they did become more like Christ as they served others. Later, at age 25, I would get hired at a church of more than 5,000 members and about 2,000 in attendance. Shockingly, I again assumed that these people would only be "quality" (whatever that means!)…I quickly surmised that these people, as well, were just as hopeless without Jesus. The difference in the church running 30 from the church running 300 is often that no one can meet the pastor's standards of what it takes to be good enough to serve in the church. The difference in the church running 300 and the church running 2,000, is simply often that the pastor has recruited more people to serve in more roles that will substantially involve them in the work of the ministry of the local church.

Some pastors think in terms of what is the minimum we need to make a ministry work, but if that thinking translates to the minimum amount of volunteers needed to operate a service, then this will hinder the possibility of more involvement of the people. Perhaps the parking lot at a small church can be manned by two people somewhat effectively. If the same parking lot could be manned by four people instead, this may produce a two-fold outcome. One, people may be greeted by twice as many happy people (making the guest feel more comfortable), and four people are involved in ministry instead of two. The other two who may have only been inactive participants the week before being involved in the ministry are now actively involved in helping people find their way to Jesus by greeting them in a local church. Something interesting happens as people working a parking lot stand and around and talk between cars. Friendship and care begin to grow, and people become a community that knows each other. These now invested church members or attendees now have a much greater likelihood of actually attending church service than if they had no commitment to do so. Additionally, the newly involved church members now have family members that are more likely to attend. Overall, these two new volunteer parking ministers increase the total attendance at church, they add to the professionalism and "got it together" feel of the church and most importantly, they may be the reason that someone who would have decided to turn around in an empty, uninviting church parking lot would decide to stay for the church service and eventually give their life to Jesus in the weeks and months to come. If a pastor said, "Well, we only need two people in the parking lot", but two additional workers in the parking lot may have a large impact on whether or not more people decide to attend the church.

The fifth idea concerning Breaking Church Growth Barriers

10.5 Read and Pay Great Attention to the Book, How to Break Growth Barriers

by Carl F. George, and Warren Bird.[167] I have been to several seminars and trainings on breaking growth barriers, read several books on the subject, have been a part of one church that grew from 280 to

---

[167] George and Bird.

upwards of 700 while I was on staff, led a church from 11 to over 400 people through the doors weekly and have ministered on staff in a church of more than 5,000 members - through my personal experience (and the experience of thousands of other pastors who agree) the book listed in this chapter is the masterpiece work in this area. Read it, study it, read it again and do it. If you are co-dependent by nature - read it many times and ask the Lord to change you.

The book specifically addresses the 200, 400, and 800 barriers. The book also goes into much greater detail about the things mentioned in this brief chapter.

The End

I hope the book has been helpful to you and your congregation or future congregation in some way. Thanks for reading it. Be blessed today and may the Lord help us grow and plant healthy churches for the Kingdom of God.

–Sincerely, In Christ, Brian

BIBLIOGRAPHY

Anonymous house church member, "Differences Between House Churches and Three- Self Churches" (Chinese Law & Government, 2017, Vol. 49, Issue 3), pp.161-163. As accessed from Business Source Complete Database, through the Harold Hunter Theological Library, Ebscohost, Accessed November 20, 2018.

ARC Launch Training Manual. April 2016. Association of Related Churches, 1201 Lee Branch Ln, Birmingham, AL 35242.

Assemblies of God. "AG Trust Assemblies of God." agtrust.org. https://agtrust.org/Initiatives (accessed April 19, 2019).

Biney, Moses O. "Building Bridges in New York City: Starting With Churches", *The Living Pulpit (Online), 24, no 1, Spring 2015, p. 14-16. as accessed November 18, 2018. through the Ebscohost, Harold Hunter Theological Library.*

Branaugh, Mark. "Willow Creek's 'huge shift': influential megachurch moves away from seeker-sensitive services." *Christianity Today*, 52, no 6, Jun 2008, p 13.

Branson, Mark Branson, and Warnes, Nicholas. 2014. *Starting Missional Churches*. Downers Grove, Illinois: Intervarsity Press.

Briggs, Megan, "How Progressives View Scripture (and Homosexuality in the Bible)", August 6, 2018, Church Leaders.com, accessed April 19, 2019, https://churchleaders.com/news/330294-homosexuality-in-the-bible-adam-hamilton-progressive-view.html.

Brown, Walter. "Home Cell Groups and House Churches" (The Theological Educator, 41 Spring 1990), pp. 203-206. As accessed from ATLA Religion Database, through the Harold Hunter Theological Library, Ebscohost, Accessed November 20, 2018.

Buntain, Ian B, "Church Planting in the Secular West: Learning from the European Experience", Themelios, 42, no 3, December 2017, p 591.

Burke, Daniel. "Mark Driscoll, top megachurch pastor, resigns", Newspaper Source Plus, CNN Wire, October 15, 2014: 227. Accessed March 25, 2019. http://web.a.ebscohost.com/ehost/detail/detail?vid=9&sid=b15ecb53-98cd-4b1d-a282-309f41d15926%40sdc-v-sessmgr03&bdata=JnNpdGU9ZWhvc3QtbGl2ZQ%3d%3d#AN=BAQ41413407195&db=n5h

Carl F. George, and Warren Bird. *How to Break Growth Barriers*. Grand Rapids, MI: Baker Books, 1993, updated 2017.

Christian Century, "Methodist Ranks Drop for 36th Straight Year", Vol. 123, Issue 10, p15. May 16, 2006, accessed April 19, 2019.

Chung, Esther, "'Reconciling' United Methodist Churches Lose Members", Juicy Ecumenism: The Institute on Religion and Democracy's Blog, March 28, 2018; accessed April 20, 2019, https://juicyecumenism.com/2018/03/28/rmn-causes-decline-united-methodist-umc-congregation/

Church of God International Offices, Church of God 74th General Assembly Minutes (Cleveland, TN: Pathway Press, 2012), 18.

Connor, Neil, "Christians outraged as China destroys mega-church", Daily Telegraph (London). 01/12/2018, p16-16. Harold Hunter Theological Library, Ebscohost, Accessed March 28, 2018. http://web.b.ebscohost.com/ehost/detail/detail?vid=5&sid=b5b19815-faa4-45ba-bf0d-138014111a0f%40pdcsessmgr03&bdata=JnNpdGU9ZWhvc3Qtb-Gl2ZQ%3d%3d#db=n5h&AN=8Q2133481005\

Crouch, Andy. "Planting deep roots: when you get serious about cultural change, you get serious about institutions" *Christianity Today*, 57, no 5, Jun 2013, p 61.

Dart, John. "Proud of the UMC Label", The Christian Century, 118, no 25, September 12-19, 2001, p. 12. Harold Hunter Theological Library, Ebscohost, Accessed December 5, 2018.

Effa, Allan, "Pub congregations, coffee house communities, tall steeple churches, and sacred space: The missional church movement and architecture", Article, Missiology, 43 no 4 Oct 2015, p.373-384. Harold Hunter Theological Library, Ebscohost, Accessed November 18, 2018.

Forrester, Mark. "AG Reaches Historic Number of New Churches", Springfield, MO: General Council of the Assemblies of God, 2017; as accessed April 19, 2019, p. 1-4, https://news.ag.org/news/ag-reaches-historic-number-of-new-churches

Gaines, Grant. "The Church as Movement: Starting and Sustaining Missional-Incarnartional Communities", Book Review, Themelios, 42 no 1 Apr 2017, p. 232-234. Harold

Godin, Seth. "'Marketing to Nobody", Seth's Blog, May 10, 2011; accessed May 10, 2019, https://seths.blog/2011/05/marketing-to-nobody/

Gregor, Allison. "How to Fill a Melting Pot", New York Times, June 11, 2013.

Grigg, Ty. book review, "Starting Missional Churches: life with God in the neighborhood" (Evangelical Missions Quarterly); 51 no 3 Jul 2015, p. 351-352, ALTA

Hadaway, C. Kirk and Penny L. Marler, "New Church Development: A Research Report" (New York: Episcopal Church Center, 2001), p 4-5; as accessed April 17, 2019 www.episcopalchurch.org/files/ncdreport2.pdf

House of Deputies Committee on the State of the Church, *"Report to the 76th General Convention, Otherwise Known as the Blue Book, Reports to the Committees, Commissions, Agencies and Boards of the General Convention of the Episcopal Church Seventy-Six General Convention, Anaheim, California, July 8-17, 2009"*, p 75, as accessed April 17, 2019. https://extranet.generalconvention.org/staff/files/download/364.pdf

Hunter Theological Library, Ebscohost, Accessed March 28, 2018.

Hyatt, Bob. abstract article "Under Discussion", Christianity Today, Vol. 53 Issue 10 (October 2009), p. 12.

Ireland, Michael. "'Chinese Authorities Blow Up Popular Megachurch", Charisma News, March 8, 2019; accessed May 10, 2019, https://www.charismanews.com/world/75499-chinese-authorities-blow-up-popular-megachurch

Jim Griffith and Bill Easum. Ten Most Common Mistakes Made by New Church Starts. St. Louis, MO: Chalice Press, 2008.

Krause, N. "Invited Commentary: Explaining the Relationship Between Attending Worship Services and Mortality- A Brief Excursion Into the Contribution of Social Relationships in Religious Institutions" (American Journal of Epidemiology; 2017 Apr 01, Vol. 185 Issue 7), pp. 523-525. accessed November 18, 2018. http://doi.org/10.1093/aje/kww180

McNeal, Reggie. *Missional Communities: the Rise of the Post-Congregational Church*, 2011. San Francisco, California: Jossey-Bass.

Merriam Webster s.v. "institution," accessed April 12, 2019, https://www.merriam-webster.com/dictionary/institution.

Moran, Dan. "'Evangelicals Once Again Dominate List of Top-growing Large UM Congregations", Juicy Ecumenism: The Institute on Religion and Democracy's Blog, November 20, 2018; accessed April 22, 2019, https://juicyecumenism.com/2018/11/20/evangelicals-dominate-list-top-growing-large-um-congregations/

No Author given. "Following Up", Christian Century. 5/9/2018, Vol. 135 Issue 10, p18-18 Harold Hunter Theological Library, Ebscohost, Accessed April 12, 2018.

Pae, Keun-joo Christine. "Negotiated or Negotiating Spaces: Korean Churches in Flushing, Queens of New York City", *Cross Currents, 58, no 3,* Fall 2008, p 456-472.

Percy, Martyn. "Restoring the Kingdom: the radical Christianity of the house church movement" (Journal of Contemporary Religion, 14 no 1 Jan 1999), pp. 157-160. Harold Hunter Theological Library, ATLA Religion Database, Accessed November 20, 2018.

Religion Database. accessed November 18, 2018.

Roberts, Sam. "Listening to (and Saving) the World's Languages", New York Times, April 29, 2010.

Shellnutt, Kate, "Hundreds of New Churches Not Enough to Satisfy Southern Baptists", Christianity Today, June 9, 2017; accessed April 19, 2019, p 2, https://www.christianitytoday.com/news/2017/june/southern-baptist-convention-churches-baptisms-sbc-acp.html

Snook, Susan Brown, "Reaching New People through Church Planting". Anglican Theological Review, 92, no 1, Winter 2010, p 111-116. ATLA Religion Database, as accessed from the Harold Hunter Theological Library, November 18, 2018.

Stetzer, Ed. 2018. "Finding the right Church Plant Model: An Introduction to Church Models (Part 1)." Edstetzer.com, December 26, 2018. Accessed February 22, 2019. https://

edstetzer.com/2018/12/finding-the-right-church-plant-model-an-introduction-to-church-models-part-1/?mc_cid=ea0deb17ed&mc_eid=0f447d78ed

Stetzer, Ed. 2019. "Finding the right Church Plant Model: The Traditional Model (Part 2)." Edstetzer.com, January 3, 2019. Accessed February 22, 2019. https://edstetzer.com/2019/01/finding-the-right-church-plant-model-the-traditional-model-part-2/?mc_cid=6d4694e95f&mc_eid=0f447d78ed

Stetzer, Ed. 2019. "Finding the right Church Plant Model Part 4: The Missional Incarnational Approach." Edstetzer.com, January 9, 2019. Accessed February 22, 2019. https://edstetzer.com/2019/01/finding-the-right-church-planting-model-part-4-the-missional-incarnational-approach/

Stetzer, Ed. 2019. "Finding the right Church Plant Model Part 5: The Organic House Church Model." Edstetzer.com, January 16, 2019. Accessed February 27, 2019. https://edstetzer.com/2019/01/finding-the-right-church-planting-model-part-5-the-organic-house- church-approach/?mc_cid=5cce7f1c-8b&mc_eid=0f447d78ed

Stetzer, Ed and Connor, Philip, *RESEARCH REPORT A Publication of the Center for Missional Research, North American Mission Board,* Center for Missional Research, 2007, accessed November 18, 2018. https://pcamna.org/churchplanting/documents/CPMainReport.pdf

Stoffer, Dale R., "Church Planting: An Anabaptist Model", Brethren Life and Thought, 39, no 3,

Summer 1994, p. 210-221. Harold Hunter Theological Library, Ebscohost, Accessed December 5, 2018.

Tino, James and Brink, Paul. "A Model for Urban Church Planting, the First Phase: From Preliminary Investigation to First Worship Service", *Missio Apostolica*, 7 Mar 1999, p 40-46.

UMData.org, "UMData, the United Methodist Church Online Directory and Statistics", General Council on Finance and Administration of the United Methodist Church, 2019; accessed April 19, 2019, "Stats" link, http://www.umdata.org/UMFactsHome.aspx

Wesley, Luke. "Is the Chinese Church Predominantly Pentecostal?." Asian Journal of Pentecostal Studies, Vol 7, Issue 2 (July 2004): 225-254. Accessed November 20, 2018. http://web.b.ebscohost.com/ehost/pdfviewer/pdfviewer?vid=4&sid=-30ca5f3c-1f0f-430a-962b-c7bacb702445%40sessionmgr104.

White, Chris. "House Church Christianity in China: From Rural Preachers to City Pastors" book review, (Studies in World Christianity, 23 no 2, 2017), p. 188-189. Accessed November 20, 2018.

White, Thomas. Professor of Theology, Southwestern Baptist Theological Seminary. abstract article "Under Discussion", Christianity Today, Vol. 53 Issue 10 (October 2009), p. 12.

Xin, Yalin, "Inner Dynamics of the Chinese house church movement: the case of the Word of Life community" (Mission Studies, 25 no 2, 2008). Accessed November 20, 2018.

www.ingramcontent.com/pod-product-compliance
Lightning Source LLC
Chambersburg PA
CBHW032108090426
42743CB00007B/281